PRAISE FOR
WOMEN GONE WILD: WEALTH

"I'm excited to see more women stepping into their power as investors
and entrepreneurs. This book will help open the doors
for more women to believe they can do it too."
—Kevin Harrington, the Original Shark from *Shark Tank*

"Tug[s] on the heartstrings of women all over the world."
—*Forbes*

"This is a diverse group of women who are wildly successful
with wildly great stories worth reading."
—*Los Angeles Tribune*

"A safe space for everyone to live authentically and speak their truth . . .
the Wealth edition was published to empower you!"
—*Authority Magazine*

"*Women Gone Wild* is not only an amazing book, it's a sisterhood of
like-minded women who want to work together and grow!
I recommend this book to any woman on any level of business."
—Heather Marianna, Founder of Beauty Kitchen

WOMEN GONE
WILD

WOMEN GONE

WILD

WEALTH

THE FEMININE GUIDE
TO FEARLESS LIVING

RHONDA SWAN
DIANA VON WELANETZ WENTWORTH

BROWN BOOKS
PUBLISHING GROUP

Women Gone Wild: Wealth
The Feminine Guide to Fearless Living

Brown Books Publishing Group
Dallas, TX / New York, NY
www.BrownBooks.com
(972) 381-0009

A New Era in Publishing®

Publisher's Cataloging-In-Publication Data

Names: Swan, Rhonda, author. | Von Welanetz Wentworth, Diana, 1941- author.
Title: Women gone wild. Wealth : the feminine guide to fearless living / Rhonda Swan,
Diana Von Welanetz Wentworth.
Other titles: Wealth : the feminine guide to fearless living
Description: Dallas, TX ; New York, NY : Brown Books Publishing Group, [2023]
Identifiers: ISBN: 9781612546360 (hardcover) 9781612546506
    (paperback) | LCCN: 2022950487
Subjects: LCSH: Wealth--Anecdotes. | Quality of life--Anecdotes. |
    Businesswomen--Anecdotes. |
Self-actualization (Psychology) in women--Anecdotes. | Success--Anecdotes.
    | LCGFT: Anecdotes. | BISAC: BUSINESS & ECONOMICS / Women in
    Business. | SELF-HELP / Personal Growth / Success.
Classification: LCC: HB251 .S93 2023 | DDC: 330.16--dc23

ISBN 978-1-61254-650-6 (PB)
ISBN 978-1-61254-636-0 (HC)
LCCN 2022950487

Printed in China
10 9 8 7 6 5 4 3 2 1

For more information or to contact the author, please go to www.WGWBook.com.

This book is dedicated to all of the WILD women of the world brave enough to tell their story. Thank you for being powerful and strong, gifted and courageous, bold and edgy, unapologetic and raw, and delivering your unmasked inner truth. I hope this book enables other women to see themselves as I see you. I believe this book will serve as a reminder for all women to know that their story matters and to reach out of their comfort zones and share it. The world is changing, and women are a big part of this change. I see women awakening and leading this change, creating a more peaceful and benevolent world.

I hope this book serves as a reminder or wake-up call for some people. We, as a society, need to create a more truthful world that places more value on the things money cannot buy over material wealth. In the end, we must all participate in creating a better, more loving and respectful world . . . one day at a time.

"If you want to see how wealthy you really are, just count all the things that money can't buy."

—Unknown

TABLE OF CONTENTS

ACKNOWLEDGMENTS   XV

INTRODUCTION   1

PART I: THE WEALTH CONNECTION

1. EXPECT MAGIC!   7
    Diana von Welanetz Wentworth

2. UNCOMMON WISDOM, UNCOMMON WEALTH   15
    Karen Whelan

3. ABUNDANCE OF INTUITION   21
    Michelle Beltran

4. PARTNERSHIPS CREATE A WEALTHY LIFE   29
    Kortney Murray

PART II: PASSION LEADS TO PURPOSE

5. WHAT YOU VALUE   39
    Hanalei Swan

6.   FROM A VISION TO A CALLING   45
     Michale Gabriel

7.   A BEAUTIFUL LIFE   51
     Adriana Monique Alvarez

8.   ABUNDANT LIVING   57
     Dana Kay

PART III: MIND, BODY, AND SPIRIT WEALTH

9.   THE NATURE OF ABUNDANCE   67
     Camberly Gilmartin

10. YOUR MILLIONAIRE KARMA   73
     Stefanie Bruns

11. THE WELL OF SOURCE IS THE SOURCE OF WEALTH   81
     Robin Mullin

12. ANCESTRAL WEALTH   87
     Genevieve Searle

13. MANIFESTING WEALTH   95
     Ania Halama

PART IV: CHOICES BECOME EMPOWERMENT

14. THE WEALTH OF PERSONAL FULFILLMENT   105
     Tarryn Reeves

15. NURTURING SUCCESS   111
     Ebony Swank

16. FREEDOM TO CHOOSE   117
     Shar Moore

17. SHARING TO EMPOWER   123
     Blair Kaplan Venables

PART V: THE PERSONAL BRAND OF YOU

18. BECOME AN ASSET   133

    Danelle Delgado

19. VISUALIZE SUCCESS   139

    April Ryan

20. SHOWING UP AS THE VIP OF YOUR OWN LIFE IN GRATITUDE   145

    Barbie Layton

21. BRAND CURRENCY WEARS THE CROWN   151

    Rhonda Swan

ABOUT THE AUTHORS   157

ACKNOWLEDGEMENTS

The world is a better place thanks to all the WILD women who are taking a stand for women all over the world to share their voice and guide our next generation of leaders. Thank you to everyone who strives to grow and help others grow into a greater version of themselves.

To all the WILD women I have had the honor to lead, be led by, or watch their leadership from afar: I want to say thank you for being the inspiration and foundation for the Women Gone Wild book series.

I have the most loving gratitude for my unstoppable family for always supporting and being by my side. Even through my WILD ideas, you are my rock. I love you, Brian and Hanalei.

Without the experiences and support from my peers and the Unstoppable team at Unstoppable Branding Agency, this book would not exist. You have given me the opportunity to lead a great group of individuals, and to be a leader of great leaders is a blessed place to be. Thank you to Yana, Amara, Araminta, Dian, Marie, Nina, Jez, Aljello, Dave, Delaine, Emily, Jelena, Mitchell, Josie, Shen, and Starr.

Having an idea and turning it into a book with twenty-two women is as hard as it sounds. The experience is both challenging and rewarding. I especially want to thank the individuals that helped make this happen. Complete thanks to our publisher Brown Books Publishing Group, especially Milli, Tom, and Sterling.

Special thanks to my dear sister Diana von Welanetz Wentworth for your unwavering guidance and support.

INTRODUCTION

Women Gone Wild is not just a fancy phrase. It's not a fleeting passion project with an expiry date. It is a movement. It is an invitation for women everywhere to rise, find their voices, and make change—for themselves, for their families, for each other, and for all of us.

The idea for *Women Gone Wild*, the first dawn of this movement, came from a need to see more women joining together and collaborating. I was at an event with fifteen other women, and we were sharing our business "secrets" and resources when we realized that we don't see women sitting at the table like this very often. We began to discuss what we could do to create change within the consciousness of women and bring them together. *Women Gone Wild* was created as a platform, a space, for women to come together and tell their stories. The Women Gone Wild series has come forward to showcase the wholesomeness of women.

This book is the first in a series of four—Wealth, Intuition, Leadership, Diversity—that dive deep into some of the key qualities that make women so powerful. Not powerful in the negative, patriarchal way, but powerful in the way of true transformation, connection, and magic. The Wealth edition is about us coming together and reclaiming the meaning of wealth, not just in a monetary or currency value, but in so many different ways, and telling others what wealth really means.

So why wealth?

Wealth is one of those touchy subjects that so many people tend to dance around. We have been conditioned to believe that "Money is the root of all evil," that wealthy people are bad, and that money is dirty. And God forbid that you openly talk about money in public! The energy and dynamics around money, wealth, and abundance needs to change—especially for women.

It is a common misconception that being rich and having lots of money means that you are wealthy. This couldn't be further from the truth. Being rich and being wealthy are two completely different things. Rich people aren't always wealthy; poor people are often wealthy. And there is every shade in between.

Wealth and how people define wealth is evolving. The creation of this book is one of the pieces within that evolution.

Wealth isn't necessarily the amount of money in your bank account, how fat your 401(k) is, how much real estate, crypto currency, mutual funds, or stocks that you own. It doesn't come down to owning your own business, how many Prada shoes you own, or the Rolex you have on your wrist. Yes, all these things have value, but these ideas of wealth are superficial and have us, as a society, trapped in the endless cycle of wanting more—do more, achieve more, buy more, and *then* you will be happy. We know that this isn't the case. Some of the most financially abundant people are the most unhappy. The feel-good hit we get when we buy the latest phone or that "better" car never lasts long, and we are left feeling empty and looking for the next hit. Why is that?

Wealth goes so much deeper than the one-dimensional, shallow perception of our societal status, much of which is currently defined by what we parade around on the outside. No. Wealth has so many layers and is accessible to all of us no matter our work title, the country we live in, or the circumstances we find ourselves in.

Some of you are probably thinking that the wealth I am referring to is time and freedom, but even those are somewhat obvious answers. It is true that money, time, and freedom can add to your wealth, but they are not the only three markers by which we can define how wealthy we are.

The highest and truest wealth isn't as simple as cash, crypto, and real estate, and it isn't as oversimplistic as time and freedom. The evolving experience of wealth, now more than ever, includes access, leverage, authentic expression, experiences, and a much deeper way of moving through and interacting with life. Real wealth is reflected in the way that you are able to show up in the world. This includes everything from your mindset to your mentors. The wealthiest people have access to everything from backstage passes with the biggest talent, doctors with the most advanced treatments, to a network of trusted people who they know will always have their back. The wealthiest people have leverage in the world that includes everything from hard-to-get resources to patented technologies to priceless experiences. The wealthiest people know that money is just one aspect of their existence and are on a mission to play full-out, at all times, and live in a way that not only fulfills themselves but also those around them.

Women Gone Wild: The Wealth Edition has rounded up an influential group of women that are wealthy in more ways than one. Their stories speak to the power of access, leverage, mindset, perspective, mentors, prosperity, mastery, and so much more. We call them Women Gone Wild because they unapologetically live life on their terms and will not let their own safe excuses or others hold them back in the fulfillment of what they know they came here to do. These women value collecting moments, not things. In their own way, they are moment millionaires. This isn't to say that they don't have traditional assets; many do, but beyond those material possessions, they have something more precious than the fattest bank account or the biggest house.

Real wealth is knowing that you could lose all your material possessions and still be okay. Real wealth is resting secure in the knowledge that if you lost all your financial assets and belongings that you could make it all back if that's what you wanted to do. A wealthy woman is one that could be picked up and dropped off in a new place, in a new industry, and rise to the top again because of her WILD ways. WILD women don't play by the rules; rather, we bend them and break them for a greater cause.

Welcome to *Women Gone Wild: The Wealth Edition*. Within these pages you will connect with women just like you who share their struggles, their triumphs, and their experiences on their journey to creating their version of a wealthy life. You will laugh. You will cry. But most of all, you will learn, grow, and be inspired to keep carving your own path on this one beautiful and WILD life.

To you, my wealthy sister,

RHONDA SWAN

PART 1

THE WEALTH CONNECTION

CHAPTER 1

EXPECT MAGIC!

DIANA VON WELANETZ WENTWORTH

—New York Times Bestselling Author of *Chicken Soup for the Soul:
101 Stories with Recipes from the Heart* and Founder of the Inside Edge

Are you feeling it? The power, the passion, the *exuberance* of feminine energy?

Women won't keep a lid on their wildness anymore, and they won't allow being female to limit the size of their bank accounts.

So many of us were taught to repress our feminine instincts. As a young girl, I was scolded and told loudness was not "ladylike." Dinner table discussions were serious. "Children should be seen and not heard." My outgoing nature was sternly squashed when I was sent alone to boarding school at the age of eight. Few other girls were there, none my age, and I felt deeply lonely wandering through the school grounds. I longed for companionship.

As time went on, such deep loneliness—my core wound—would become my driving force and my greatest gift. Those dark times would lead me to create a wealth of connections and community beyond my imagining.

MAGIC ON THE HORIZON

My favorite childhood times were listening to radio shows in the car or watching television shows with personalities like Uncle Miltie and Red Skelton—times when my family would all laugh together. What a feeling of mutual enjoyment! Using practical jokes, riddles, humor, and magic tricks, I learned to spark delight in my serious family and schoolmates.

My mother and her mother, who ran a boarding house, spent lots of time in the kitchen. What warmth, fun, and generosity they shared while preparing delicious food! I loved being in the kitchen with them, perusing recipes, planning menus, preparing treats... The most fun was anticipating what pleasure it would bring. Chopping and prepping, sautéing and simmering, I was stirring blessings into every bite. I read cookbooks like novels from cover to cover and planned parties in my head.

But more than telling jokes or hosting amazing parties, I yearned for a future romantic partner who would be my forever love. I sensed how fulfilling deep intimacy would feel. I just knew I would find a way to share my whole heart. I would finally feel completely at home.

At the age of twenty-one, without warning, I had a flash of insight and broke up with the approved "eligible bachelor" I'd been dating. I wasn't feeling the kind of love I dreamed of as a kid, and at the last minute, tagged along with my parents on their long-planned tour of Asia. For the next three weeks, I felt sure I'd made the right decision. My hunches had often proved dependable, and I sensed something magical on the horizon.

Hong Kong was our final stop. I didn't notice that a man in the dining room had followed me to the elevator, only to have it close before he could step in. I woke very early the next morning, way too early to meet my parents for breakfast. I chose an elegant dress to wear (as if for a special occasion), went downstairs, and stood in the middle of the lobby.

What am I doing here so early?

Paul von Welanetz stepped out of the elevator, and I found out.

"Where are you from?"

With those words, my longed-for heart's companion had arrived. Three days later, we were engaged.

Paul and I married, and we were overjoyed with our romance and partnership.

FEELING OUR WAY INTO OUR FUTURE

I'd always loved cooking; gathering people around the table to connect with and enjoy each other made my heart sing. Thanks to Julia Child, massive interest in French cooking and entertaining took hold in America. During the first years of our marriage, I attended classes with the head chef of the Escoffier Room in Beverly Hills.

I'd always believed I was destined to become a mom, so Paul and I were thrilled to be expecting a baby. Our daughter, Lexi, was born, and along with her a complete change in my world and my personality. Little was known then about postpartum depression and the self-loathing that accompanies it. Maternal instincts just didn't kick in. I found myself housebound and quite terrified there was something very wrong with me.

Adding to my distress, I suddenly quit smoking for my new baby's sake. One fateful day while Lexi was napping, I needed to keep my hands busy so I wouldn't light a cigarette. I went into a frenzy of cooking crêpes—two pans on the fire and stacks of buttered ones covered my kitchen counters. Friends dropped by, fascinated, and asked me to teach them.

When Paul saw how excited and joyful I was to be gathering people in the kitchen, he encouraged me and bought folding tablet arm chairs to increase the seating capacity. That's how my home cooking classes began, and how I first experienced the power of being financially independent. Paul, an artist, found he also loved to present food and table decor in imaginative ways and often joined in teaching classes. He would often say, "First, you eat with your eyes!"

The timing of America's great interest in home entertaining worked in our favor, and our shared passion for teaching cooking grew into a groundbreaking career. Our first book, *The Pleasure of your Company,* won the French Tastemaker Cookbook of the Year award in the category of entertainment. Five more books followed, along with our cooking school on the Hollywood Sunset Strip, where Wolfgang Puck and other rising chefs taught. We traveled and taught classes as headliners of newspaper food festivals in Milwaukee and Toledo to audiences of at least 4,500. We were gathering not only dinner guests, but also audiences of thousands through appearances on such shows as *Good Morning America.*

Los Angeles Magazine featured Paul and me as one of LA's most romantic couples. We even hosted an early television cooking show on the Lifetime Network, *The New Way Gourmet.*

And then, as happens with trends, it all fell apart. By 1985, women entered the workforce in droves and lost interest in spending hours at the stove.

Paul and I were feeling pressured. We couldn't think of a way other than cooking to make a living. I worried and paced the floor, impatient to know *now* what our new direction could be. I knew there was magic that came out of dark times—I'd experienced it twice—but I still felt desperate. I erupted wildness to its full force and prayed fiercely, not politely, insisting on knowing our next step.

A WHOLE NEW COMMUNITY

Outside of our occupation, Paul and I had always found ourselves drawn toward seminars in personal growth. We both meditated, attended lectures and workshops, and read avidly.

A friend told us about Impact, a motivational seminar for people in the entertainment industry. It was a place where reinvention and futuristic thinking thrived. One of the many challenges was the unusual meeting times—daily from 6:00 a.m. to 8:00 a.m. and most full weekends! We committed to the cost and our nine-month stint was life changing. Several hundred of us were coaxed into setting nearly impossible goals and were held accountable to achieve them. In our first three-week initiation period, we approached a housewares vendor and raised $100,000 for a department cooking video project and actually completed our fifth cookbook, *LA Cuisine*.

As we focused on action, magic multiplied.

Through our association with Impact, Paul and I were invited to be in a documentary on citizen diplomacy at the height of the Cold War. Paired with Soviet Union chefs during a time when our governments were not speaking was terrifying: our rooms were bugged, police barged into our cabins, our motives were questioned every day. But through this experience and the people we met, we realized we were in an environment that sparked deep connections and empowerment.

At the same time, we gained appreciation for observing and listening to our fellow travelers, activists, and leaders in human potential. We marveled at how the group rallied support for our cause and for each other, making what would become lifelong connections. We realized we'd been participating in a "playground" that sparked deep connection and empowerment.

BREAKTHROUGH

We were astonished when it dawned on us that our passion had never truly been all about food. What we'd been doing was creating community environments! After that trip, Paul and I asked ourselves how we could connect crowds and create community on a grander scale by offering larger, more meaningful gatherings. Parties with a purpose!

Power breakfasts and networking events were just beginning to take place in New York. People were eager to network in new ways to enhance their business, and the group of eighty travelers we were with wanted to expand their passion for creating a better world. Inspired by the early morning hours of Impact, the Inside Edge—a weekly breakfast at the Beverly Hills Hotel—was launched. We adopted a theme of providing life-enhancing information, and our first speaker was one of our fellow travelers—American futurist Barbara Marx Hubbard.

Our weekly breakfasts with compelling speakers, table discussion topics, and live entertainment caught on. Inside Edge breakfasts spread to Orange County and to San Diego, attracting entrepreneurs and futuristic thinkers. It wasn't long before we attracted almost one thousand members.

Besides providing the morning meetings, Paul and I hosted imaginative, even more challenging dinner parties for our members.

COME AS YOU WILL BE IN FIVE YEARS

The invitation for one evening party declared you would dress the part of your future self, announce your achievements, and stay in character throughout the night. Dr. Susan Jeffers stepped out of a limousine holding three mock books and proclaimed she had just returned from her third *New York Times* bestseller tour. Her first book, *Feel the Fear and Do It Anyway,* soon became a massive bestseller, followed by two more. She achieved what she'd announced! So did many others. The law of attraction, of creating vivid feelings before achieving what you wish for, was standard practice at The Inside Edge. It was a place where you could both imagine and manifest the wealth you desired, where you could expect magic!

Magic continued to manifest through us and all those around us as Paul and I continued to connect and help others discover their own version of wealth.

MY NEW LOVES

Paul, just after our twenty-fifth anniversary in 1988, was diagnosed with terminal cancer. We were devastated by the news. I promised to keep the Inside Edge meetings going. Shortly before he passed, Paul surprised me by saying, "I don't want you to be alone."

"Send me someone!" I blurted.

"I will!" he declared.

He did. Only a few months later, Ted Wentworth walked right into my life and my heart at the Inside Edge, bringing me thirty-one more years of marital bliss. Here was another example of asking for and being willing to accept new, different results when in the middle of a dark time.

One morning in the early nineties, I sat with Jack Canfield and Mark Victor Hansen as they brainstormed their concept for the Chicken Soup for the Soul book series. It wasn't long until the first two books in the series held the top two positions on the *New York Times* bestseller lists. The publisher was approached by the Shopping Network for an exclusive debut of the *Chicken Soup for the Soul Cookbook*. Magically, I became the first coauthor in the series with the third book. I was forced to develop my story writing skills and loved that I would be positioned in the food world again with offers to present cooking lectures on cruise ships.

Recently, at the Inside Edge's thirty-fifth anniversary gala in 2021, Jack Canfield remarked that without the Inside Edge, Chicken Soup for the Soul, once the largest selling book series of all time (half a billion sold!), may never have come into being.

Years with Teddy sped by, and my delight in creating events and parties never waned. My romantic memoir, *Send Me Someone: A True Story of Love Here and Hereafter,* tells the story.

REAL MAGIC!

Here I am, at eighty-one, widowed for the second time, not just expecting, but being flooded with more magic than ever! Though I deeply miss Ted's affection, his encouragement, his playful wit, I now savor solitude—and an entirely new sense of sovereignty to explore.

You see, now that I'm alone, I don't really need to behave myself. I can loudly insist on magic! Order in a miracle! Being open to different ideas in dark times has led me to wealth and people I could never have imagined. Now I invite guidance into my life. Where can I inspire the most joy today? What magical step lies ahead? How happily abundant, how wildly wonderful, can my life become?

Try it and expect magic!

—*DIANA*

CHAPTER 2

UNCOMMON WISDOM, UNCOMMON WEALTH

KAREN WHELAN

—Founder of Solution Therapy

Living in creation is fearless living. How many of us can say we have walked the terrain of our inner abyss and found our way home—home to the truth of ourselves? This is the wealth that I have come to know. A wealth that is not defined by financial success, but one that unshackles you from living your life based on how society defines you. You can have money in the bank and be broken inside, with little or no happiness or inner peace. The way to inner peace is when you are happy and accept the truth about who you are. To know it and live it is enriching.

There is a wisdom deep within you, buried under the opinions, stories, and beliefs about yourself that you inherited through your relationships with family members and peers. You became a version of a "self" based on these inherited beliefs you identified with. Either your story about yourself is loving, self-accepting, and self-supportive, or you see yourself as unworthy.

You can also apply this phrase when it comes to this uncommon wealth, because to not know your spiritual being is to be in debt to life and the systems that are set up against your authentic self. Richness is being able to taste the essence of your presence and celebrate the mystery and wonderment of being alive inside of yourself. You are not seeking permission or validation from others, but instead are living up to your fullest potential. You are free to be you, uninhibited—this is fearless living! That, to me, is what wealth is all about.

When you're not living your authentic self, that is pure deprivation. "Life," according to my spiritual teacher, Derek O'Neill, "is not meant to hurt you; it's meant to wake you up to the truth of who you are."

A SHRINKING WORLD

I discovered how unsafe the world was from a very young age. I endured a childhood trauma that saw me turn against myself and brought me on a journey of self-hate and self-sabotage. I began to lose myself to a deep pain that I could not resolve inside of me. Instead, I became buried in self-hate; my trust and love in myself and the world had shrunk. My self-hate intensified, and I began hating my physical form and attempted to take my life at fifteen. When I woke in the hospital bed the day after my overdose, I was disappointed that I was still here, trapped inside a being I wanted so desperately to be rid of! This hate of my body continued into my twenties. I would compare my body to other women and always find something wrong with myself. I could not sit comfortably in my body; I would pull at my clothes in agitation while beating myself up emotionally. I became paranoid around others, believing that they could only see my ugliness, my fatness. I believed this because when I looked at myself, I was looking from wounded eyes. When I only saw ugliness, I believed others saw it too.

At that point in my life, due to my cynical outlook, I had no sense of anything spiritual. I numbed my true depth by not caring about anything except what others thought of me.

I was disconnected from myself, and in essence, I was disconnected from the Divine (or God, or however you choose to identify it). My spiritual intelligence knows that this divine aspect is within all of us. We are not disconnected from it; it is within us, waiting for us to remember it is there. When you know it, this is when you are born out of humanity and into divinity! For me, this is self-love: a way of being that brings forth a richness in how we experience and engage with our lives. Disconnecting from the Divine saw me doubt myself and cultivate a scarcity mindset, in which I saw absence and impossibility in everything.

Your life shouldn't be about maintaining the status quo by having a big house, fancy car, and some idealized, perfect family based on what society tells you. If you are trying to make it in the world, competing against everyone else just to be and feel like somebody, then it's all ambition without purpose. I was a woman who truly believed I would be happy when I got to those milestones: when I had the house, the money, and the man. I truly believed in all of this and chased it for years! My mindset at the time was that I could only be happy when I could check all of these boxes perfectly.

Can you identify with this?

This is how it was for me when I never felt worthy or good enough. I believed that I needed to be everything in order to be accepted.

I lived on the edge for a couple of years; when I was sixteen, I was either sleeping on the streets or numbing my pain with drugs. But one day, I felt an existential call to adventure and decided to heed it. Months later, I was on a plane heading to France to become an au pair—despite the fact that I spoke no French. While there, I discovered that the French mother I worked for was also a healer. When I crashed my scooter, cracking my ribs and breaking my fingers, she placed her hands over my ribs and over my hand. I briefly felt nausea, but then calmness entered my heart, and the pain was gone. My ribs and hand were perfect. She gazed intensely into my eyes, informing me, "You have a lot of trauma and anger in this body. You need to learn about forgiveness and how to let go!"

She taught me about the power of forgiveness and how holding on to hate will manifest as illness in the body. Through her guidance, I learned to soften towards myself and to see myself with a different "story." Instead of blaming myself for everything, I developed compassion for all I endured and experienced. This was a turning point! I began to work and heal the parts of myself that had learned to be a victim and suffer. I sat down with a therapist and learned to accept myself. I showed up in a therapy chair every week and did so for the next eleven years before starting to train as a therapist myself. I was now on a mission to truly know myself in a deep way.

THE INNER AWAKENING

Now my life began to take shape; I was growing beyond the old version of "Karen." The more I discovered myself in therapy, the more conscious I became of how I shape and impact my world. I realized that we cannot control what comes our way, but we have real control of our inner reactions and how we respond to situations as they unfold.

After France, and after I gave birth to my son, I decided I wanted to go to college and become a psychotherapist. I knew I could because I had begun to trust in myself, which provided a deep inner safety. I recognized that the more I know myself, the less afraid I was of the world. I returned to education and studied for ten consecutive years. During college, I fell in love and had a beautiful daughter. We were happy! But my soul kept evolving, and I felt the call within me again, wanting me to expand more in my life. I started to nurture and embrace my creative side. At the suggestion of a life coach, I went and played in screen acting and drama classes. This environment allowed me to express and discover myself in ways I never had before.

I went deep into myself through daily meditations, seeking to discover more of my psyche through silent retreats and water fasting. Grief was there; it was actually always there in a subtle way within my heart. I sat with my heart, asking the pain what it needed, and discovered the following revelation:

I was doing everything for everybody else and would abandon myself to people-please. I did it to be liked because I had rejected myself so much and learned to put more value on what people thought of me. My inner frame of reference was: it matters what I think you think of me! I understood that I did this to survive the fear of rejection. When we people-please, we do it primarily to feel validated. Unfortunately, placing so much importance on what others think of you results in you living a life in fear and physical discomfort. Once I understood this mindset, I was unshackled from it and felt emotionally lighter. I was not used to attending to myself; I had always been there for other people, doing whatever I could to make their lives comfortable. Now it was my turn to prioritize myself and give myself this same level of energy and care.

This was a period of great metamorphosis, like a cocooned caterpillar emerging as a beautiful butterfly. When you take a closer look, you can see that the caterpillar has no idea that it's destined to be a butterfly, but the intelligent cells know. The behavior of the caterpillar changes, and it cocoons itself in preparation to become the butterfly.

When you recognize you cannot change what life may bring, but you have real power in how you choose to deal with the situation you, too, can create a transformation of this degree. You can always change your environment, whether that is doing a new activity, going somewhere different, or experiencing something new. Once your circumstances change, it's likely that a hidden aspect within you will emerge. This might be a new skill or a new mindset. Invest in you, whether that means taking a yoga class, starting a personal development course, or doing an activity that taps into your creative side. Investing in yourself will build a new sense of trust in your identity.

As for me, I decided to reframe my story and see that the soul was meant for the journey it endured. That is what I teach my clients today: to hold forgiveness and compassion for their humanity. This informs my work as a psychotherapist, tantric teacher, and energy healer. In other words, I do short-term transformational therapy and take interest in helping people connect to their authentic selves. I work with teens and adults and offer sessions, workshops, and retreats. I am a soul whisperer where your soul tells me what's going on. Our souls cocreate the pathway home.

I know the dark night of the soul, and I know the internal work it takes to heal. I have been a psychotherapist for over fifteen years now, and I see how by supporting a person to become more conscious of their pain, they can use it as a conduit to discover their true nature. They find this incredible acceptance of who they are, and they become comfortable within themselves to the point that they become liberated in their lives. Like birds leaving the nest, they take off, living fearlessly!

TRUE WEALTH

Worth is often understood as an external validation based on the material and financial attainments in your life. However, if these are lost, then that worth attached to them also goes. True wealth is found in the divine self within. This value does not go away if physical wealth does, because the wealth I am speaking of is self-worth. You do not lose your true inner source when you lose money or material objects. The wealth of self-acceptance is permanent.

I see now that my struggles were meant to be used as a tool for me to dig deep within my identity, leading to massive transformation and growth. I came to see it as a miracle opportunity. Life will always happen—we cannot avoid it—but I now know that I have full power and control over how I respond to any crisis. No matter the difficulty I encountered, I always found the answer once I looked within. This is something you can do too. Try not to become lost in the experience, but ask, "What is this experience trying to teach me?"

In my experience, we find wealth in truly knowing ourselves. If we are fully in tune with our divine selves, we will find our worthiness. To me, this worthiness is uncommon wealth. To find it, spend time with yourself. Journal your experiences. Prioritize *you* and do what makes you happy. You are here to be you, not anyone else. If you must discover yourself first, then start there. Your self-worth is a hidden treasure that is worth finding.

— *KAREN*

CHAPTER 3

ABUNDANCE OF INTUITION

MICHELLE BELTRAN

—Bestselling Author of *Take the Leap: What It Really Means to be Psychic*
and Host of *The Intuitive Hour: Awaken Your Inner Voice*

We all know that wealth is the measurement of what our combined assets are worth. It is the physical possessions we own and what can be converted into a form used for transactions. It is something we can hold, bargain with, and count. However, there is a secret source of wealth we can't hold, a wealth we already own and utilize as though it is a physical asset. It is often the one stable thing that influences how, when, and where we will acquire physical wealth.

It is our intuition, our subconscious mind. The power inherent in our subconscious mind is something we should include in our list of valuable possessions. You see, it is quite possible that the powers generated by our subconscious are more valuable than the physical things we own.

Intuition—a bridge between our conscious and subconscious minds—exists alongside our sensations, thoughts, and emotions. Balancing these faculties enables us to maximize our potential and make decisions that will contribute to our overall well-being.

Intuition is a form of knowledge that materializes in our consciousness without deliberation. It works without our knowing it. It is just there when the situation calls for it. It is not magical. It is a faculty generated by the unconscious mind that delivers hunches and prods us to act and/or reevaluate. Our intuition rapidly sifts through our past experiences and accumulated knowledge to give us an accurate assessment of any situation or decision we may have to make.

SUBCONSCIOUS PROTECTION

Intuition is the wealthy component of our spirit that protects and advises us when there is no other mechanism for deciding. It is our gift for being human. Like everything in life, you must acknowledge intuition and use it, or it will become too faint to hear. The more you listen to your intuition, and the more you act on what it suggests, the more heightened your awareness will become. Your intuition is the strongest connection you will have to your subconscious mind.

I learned how to link these two mental functions when I realized it gave me unprecedented access to the source of all creativity, wisdom, and understanding. It is the link to a new and extraordinary kind of thinking, and I wanted a piece of that.

GUT SENSING

Have you ever planned to do something but stopped because of a gut feeling, a premonition, or a sense something is about to happen? That's your intuition. It is often called a sixth sense, instinct, percipient, a hunch, second sight, or just a feeling.

One of the most famous intuitive episodes was experienced by President Abraham Lincoln. He told of a dream he had that was filled with the sounds of mourners. Lincoln followed the weeping and crying to the White House, where he found guards stationed near a casket. Lincoln asked a guard who had died. The reply was, "The president. He was killed by an assassin." The account appeared in the writings of Lincoln's close friend and biographer, Ward H. Lamon, before Lincoln was fatally shot in Ford's Theatre.

I didn't realize at first that my intuition was such a useful resource. But when I learned to tune into it, it guided me in discerning the honesty and trustworthiness of a person or situation. It is intuition that makes us look twice at something or someone and lets us sense when something is off. We call that hinky, which is another way of saying that your intuition is working.

We must learn to be quiet and let that intuition speak to us. It does have our best interests at heart. If we can get out of our own way, put away the self-doubt, and just listen, we will be amazed at what we can learn.

It is quite possible that intuition is hardwired into us as a species. Intuition is closely aligned with self-preservation in nearly every situation we encounter. Surely our ancestors wouldn't have survived very long if they didn't listen to those feelings and urges that told them when a food source was near, or when they were about to be pounced on by a saber-toothed tiger.

PONDER THIS

Take a moment now to consider your past few days. Have messages of knowing, hunches, or hinky feelings emerged? Let that memory come in. Don't look for it. Don't search for it. Let it find you. Did you have a feeling that someone you had not seen for some time would call and then receive a call from them? Did you find yourself saying "I knew it" after an event? Was there an unexplained inner knowledge about a decision you had to make? Did the perfect words or artistic inspiration come to you at just the right moment with a feeling of exuberance or excitement?

Perhaps, out of what seemed like nowhere, you had an inspired idea that resolved a particular issue of importance. That's you listening to your inner knowledge. That's the start. That's your intuition guiding you.

INNER WEALTH

We seldom realize that all financial wealth has a ripple effect affecting who we are on a broader level. Our financial success in life is rooted in our thoughts, beliefs, and perspectives about money. It colors the choices we make, how we think about things, the perspectives we hold, and the belief systems passed on to us that we allow or don't allow in. Through our own self-actualization, spiritual and emotional clarity, and awareness, we can have the life of wealth we seek on all levels— not just financial.

Are you in a wealthy state of mind? The state of mind begins by holding a sense of abundance within your thinking and being. You hold abundance in your life right now. What is that? Your intuition is embedded deep within you, ready to guide you. Are you ready to tap into it and all its power? A deep-seated feeling of abundance extends far beyond the stock market. It is not an emotion to put on or a burst of energy that comes to us. It is the peace of knowing that what we possess is enough.

Some years back, everything in my life came to a screeching halt. I describe it as utter chaos. I lost a job with the state of Nevada, a twelve-year relationship was ending, I was smack-dab in the middle of chronic fatigue from having professionally raced a bicycle for many years, I didn't own a car, and I was sleeping on my mother's living room floor. I had only one way to go: within.

Like anyone who has survived chaos, I came out of it a changed person. I knew I had only three choices: I could embrace the change that was happening, modify it, or refuse it.

I embraced the change and realized a few more things in the process:

1. I realized that humor was the best way to refrain from taking myself and life so seriously. While that may seem trite, it was ever so true. I now have a favorite coffee mug on my desk with a simple statement baked in that makes me smile and reminds me to lighten up and not take life so seriously.

2. I discovered that pure positivity leads to optimism. I harnessed hope and changed my mindset. Change is indeed part of life. Sometimes it's barely noticed, and sometimes it roars through our lives like a berserk freight train. Sometimes it's pleasant and encouraging, and sometimes it's difficult and discouraging. But it is always present. It is a reality of life we cannot escape. I decided to embrace change as a reality and lean into it with a positive attitude. I knew I had choices and could manage change no matter how easy or challenging it might be.

3. I began to trust myself. I began to evaluate what matters in my life and to forget those things society told me to value. I looked to those who loved me and sought out those I could love. I sought to find the very thing Marie Kondo, the organizational guru, insists that we treasure—joy. Today, I find that in my work with clients, friends, and others who listen to their inner selves. I find it in giving and finding out what the right thing is for me. In other words, I found freedom and self-determination in the things not valued as financial wealth. This, for me, became wealth. Now, life could really begin. I found the pot of gold. It started with going within and listening to my inner voice—my intuition.

MY WEALTH STEPS

It is an understanding of true wealth that allows us to usher in financial wealth. When we are shaken to our core, we are motivated to change. On the heels of a very challenging time, I launched my business. Year one found the business producing a six-figure income—a tall order for one woman. I believe this happened because I found true wealth first. I was not seeking financial wealth. In fact, only when I found true wealth did financial wealth find me. Here are two steps I took to create financial freedom, and it's not quite what you might be thinking:

1. **Face It.** Get real with yourself and face the truth of your life. That means being honest about what is real in your life at this moment and using that information to guide the choices you make. Do an honest financial and spiritual assessment of your life today. Do an honest evaluation of your beliefs about money, the people who surround you, and the people who are important to you today. Identify where you are and where you should be, and either embrace it or change it. Life is not meant for amassing oodles of stuff or sacrificing meaningful relationships and life experiences to gain security or fame. I decided I would not regret spending time with the people I love and realized there is no material item to which I wanted to be tethered.

2. **Surrender Mindset.** It's human nature and somewhat innate to want control. It feels safe. I encourage you to surrender. Control is a myth. We never really have control. There is always something bigger than us—the bank really owns the house, job security only exists at the behest of an employer, and a life tomorrow is not promised to us. Once you begin to embrace the surrender mindset, an interesting thing happens: you feel freedom. You begin to see the benefits of surrendering your fears, ego, perfect plans, and the illusion of control. I certainly did. I found that the moment I dropped my attempts to control everything, plan for every possible scenario, and to dwell on past transgressions, my life leaped forward in an instant.

WHEN TRUE WEALTH ARRIVES

True wealth arrives when you have made the conscious choice to live life on your own terms. Living life on your own terms is what complete freedom is all about. Learn to balance your heart and your mind to manifest the life you deserve. Financial freedom and wealth are meaningless without this.

Remember it's not the financial wealth you're after. In fact, it's not even the concept of money that pushes you to want money. What you and all of us are really after is the freedom to do as we please, when we please. Money is merely the vehicle to bring us to that state of financial freedom.

True wealth and real financial freedom are having the latitude and the choice to enjoy the time that brings the most joy into your life.

To be wealthy in life is to know yourself and to be guided by your own voice within—your intuition. From this, joy and so much more are at your fingertips. It also involves appreciating what it means to be human: being present in the moment for those you love and for those who need your love. To be wealthy is to be self-aware, to live with purpose, and to be committed not only to one's own happiness but also to the happiness of others.

Looking back at my childhood, I believe that growing up in an accepting environment where spiritual concerns were commonplace made it easy to explore the important role my subconscious and my intuition played in my life. I learned early that the spiritual part of us does not exist by accident. The unspoken urge that prompts us to be wary or to explore an idea is not accidental. The foundation for being wealthy beyond our expectations is laid by who we are, inside and out.

Is wealth having a private jet, a dream home, or an expensive car? Of course not. We know better than to measure wealth by those standards. We know those things don't necessarily bring us wealth. Things are merely an indicator of monetary wealth—a wealth that may or may not be satisfying.

So today, reach for the dreams you didn't think were possible, and begin manifesting and creating your life—the life you were meant to live, a life that makes you and those around you feel alive and fulfilled. Embracing your intuition is much simpler than we might think. Remember that if something brings you joy, welcome it in. That is the first step in listening to your intuition. If you can do this, then wealth, on all levels, is yours. So look for that joy in all you do.

— *MICHELLE*

CHAPTER 4

PARTNERSHIPS CREATE A WEALTHY LIFE

KORTNEY MURRAY

—Founder and CEO of Coastal Kapital LLC

My knowledge of wealth started with my upbringing, and I am not talking about wealth from monetary things. Although my parents provided a very stable life for my brother and me, they taught us much more than the value of a dollar. I never fully grasped the foundation I was blessed with until I was older.

Growing up I was taught that having a good education leads to a good career with benefits, you know, the "American way." My mother stayed home to raise my brother and me and supported all our activities—from schooling to sports and everything in between. My mother was raised as the youngest of six, her father a factory worker and mother a homemaker. Not only did they farm their food and raise chickens, but they managed to raise a family that stayed close throughout their lives, understanding the importance of "making it work."

My father was a self-starting entrepreneur that I don't believe ever missed a day of work. He was an attorney, which took many years to accomplish due to his choppy and unstable upbringing by his grandmother, "Teta," who was from Lebanon and didn't speak a lick of English. My father was the man that showed up not only for others, but also himself. The foundation of my integrity and understanding of my wealth came from him.

THE WEALTH OF FAMILY

Both of my parents' upbringings molded what I like to call the Wealth of Family and Trust: the beginning of understanding your true values and how to use family, friends, and relationships as resources to generate wealth. My parents taught both my brother and me to never burn a bridge, hold our heads high with integrity and honesty, and when you do, you will never have to look over your shoulder. We learned to always find a way to get along no matter what. Over the years, we have become great friends and created a bond that is everlasting. Enriched by a healthy and strong bond, Ryan and I are now able to watch each other grow in success. Not only do I look up to my brother in a business role and am able to exchange ideas about business with him, but we also help each other strive to be our very best in life. The bond of family is something that will always be a strength of mine, and I am lucky in that sense.

Working hard to make something of myself was simply in my blood, and being a woman from a highly dominant patriarchal family was what always drove me to succeed. I wanted to show the world from a young age that I could do anything I set my mind to. I was pushed to go to college by my parents, but a degree was not exactly what I thought I wanted. I knew that college was the only thing my parents would help financially (and emotionally) support, and most of my friends were attending universities. I did want to experience my own world and not allow myself to sit inside a box of limitations, so I chose Northwood University, about two hours from home. I packed my car and headed to college to experience the rocky waters of becoming an independent woman on my own two feet.

BEAUTIFUL RHINO

When I got to college, I felt free. I was in my own element of making decisions; not all good decisions, but they were mine. During these days, I discovered how it felt to be financially poor, but was I really poor? I had built relationships with a group of women that made me feel wealthy beyond my financial status. We had no money but always found a way together. We helped each other with rides, food, laundry, class, but more than that, we became family. It was the abundance of wealth that my family had always taught me to believe in even when the grass is not green. The next lesson I learned—about never burning a bridge—I ended up learning the hard way.

My long-time college friend and roommate Rebecca and I had a falling out over something so minor that today I cannot even recall what it was. We lost so much time because of such a small difference, and it created a gap in our group. I will never get that time back. In 2012, we finally came to our senses, let go of our hardened hearts, and ended the ten-year silence. That apology helped bridge our friendship which made me who I am today. Rebecca passed away from a grueling battle with breast cancer during COVID-19. I am thankful we were able to rekindle our friendship beforehand.

A motto I live by is Beautiful Rhino, meaning have thick skin, don't move backwards, and hold your head high. Don't let the hardships of your past define you, but instead use them to create growth. Forgiveness gave me a newfound freedom and allowed me to deepen my relationships with others. In redefining yourself and understanding your capacity for growth, there is an abundance of wealth.

OPEN SEA OF ENTREPRENEURSHIP

My first position after college is where I started to form a method I teach to my staff today— Always Be Interviewing (the ABI Method). No matter what you do in life, you are interviewing potential relationships—from significant others to business partners. I believe if you have the ABI in place, you won't find yourself crying over spilt milk. Sales teaches you strategies such as the law of averages, fear of loss, and a sense of urgency, but the ABI teaches you to take control of your life and find the relationships that serve you. Like building a pipeline in sales, ABI gets you more quality clients, which will become the collaborating partners that move you forward in life.

With my first entrepreneur experience upon me, little did I know I would be operating a clothing store. When I was in middle school, I remember signing up for shop class because I thought I was going to learn how to "shop" and use a credit card. High fashion was always important to me at a young age, since it is the one of the only things you have as a child to set yourself apart from the others. Making a statement was important to me, and forward fashion was my love. I felt I was destined to work in retail.

One day, I walked into a clothing store called the CooCoo Caterpillar. The owner at the time was eight months pregnant and overheating from the brutal California sun. When I started shopping and sharing my love for fashion, she saw the passion in my eyes and quickly asked if I had an interest in buying her store. Although my financial offerings were strapped, I lit up; I knew I wanted this opportunity. I may not have known how to operate the cash register, but I knew how to make people look and feel beautiful.

I rounded up my friends and family and started making the store my own. I didn't have a clue where to get clothes to sell, so I started upselling TJ Maxx products until I found my way. I found the name KAOS to be fitting, as I am Kortney with a "K" and it was my first step onto the rocky boat of the open sea of entrepreneurship. Partnerships do create a large role here and, since I had not built one in the small business community, I started from the beginning learning how to buy, how to negotiate, and seeing which family and friends I could count on to assist. Unfortunately, I had not established relationships with the bank or credit companies, forcing me to bootstrap the store on my own. Due to lack of money, the store ended up undercapitalized, and I had to close my doors. The failure led me to realize that small business owners face enormous financial challenges, many of which are often hidden from them until it's too late. Partnerships and integrity are what I had left after the store crumbled. Leaning on the strategy of ABI helped me pick up the pieces.

Throughout life I had general knowledge of finance and credit, but until the end of KAOS, I had not known the importance of both. I started to understand the use of Other People's Money (OPM) with my next career move in business financing. The art of OPM holds true significance in my current life as I teach people how vital this rule is. My first entrepreneurial endeavor didn't work out due to lack of heart, but because of lack of understanding the different arms of financing for business. I bet most of you do not know that you DO NOT have to comingle your personal assets to start, equipt, or grow your business. Your personal credit score can be saved from the extra debt and credit pulls. You can work with an advocate who understands your plan.

UNDERSTANDING MYSELF

As my knowledge of the industry grew, so did my passion for serving up superior customer service and relationship lending. I knew I wanted to do things my way, which inevitably led me to form my own company in 2007, Farhat Leasing LLC—the springboard to what is known today as Coastal Kapital LLC. We create a wealth of knowledge, expansion, and business all from creating partnerships that last a lifetime. We specialize in people at Coastal Kapital, and that is something that will carry us through our lifetime.

It was time for me to deepen my strengths of management and self-healing. I had to look inward to really understand myself. I lost my father in 2015 which impacted my life deeply. To honor him, I started embracing what I love, which helped me to heal. He believed in helping people, he was empathetic and strong. Following his beliefs, I focused on educating women to find other arms of financing, understanding OPM, ABI, and walking with integrity. Women who uplift other women are unstoppable, and we all need more of that in our lives. How do I create healthy relationships with women that don't tear each other down? To start, I had to really dig in and understand myself.

I needed something to help me fill the void of balance in my life. I decided to try something that spoke to my soul, something that required unveiling of oneself and connections with women on a much higher frequency than friendship. So, in 2017, I decided to get certified in yoga. Yoga was healing, self-reflective, and, at the same time, it was a team, partnership, and love. It gave me the balance I was looking for to deepen my understanding of why I do what I do. I was able to not only gain better knowledge of empathy, but also understand what things in life didn't move me forward. This helped create space for more wealth in my life. When you have a strong circle of positive energy and you are serving people with authentic intentions, you generate wealth internally and wealth all around you.

My passion started to become clear. I wanted to become not just a wealthier business owner in all aspects, but I also wanted to give back by mentoring other women, including friends, business owners, and the community. I started by joining the American Association of Commercial Financing Brokers (AACFB) to serve my equipment financing industry. This gave me a voice to help change and create for our future. I was able to start teaching at a higher level, assist growth for entrepreneurs, and have other opportunities start opening for me. I was asked to coauthor this book, which has brought me more internal wealth and abundance of external wealth than I could ever imagine. I have formed a mutual sisterhood with each and every one of the authors, which in turn has led to collaborations and growth.

I have since created a program at Coastal Kapital that serves and assists authors in their journey to tell their stories. For women with over two years of business experience and a solid revenue stream and story, we help with their media costs to get their stories out. The program also helps these women entrepreneurs by advocating for more knowledge and tools to help them grow, such as helping them get consultations in any industry and providing access to our eBook download and podcasts on business growth.

I have chosen to create a culture in our staff that welcomes laughter and close relationships, accompanied by the expectation that they are working hard and creating new opportunities consistently. I hire family and friends that I trust to help grow our business because we feel the same when it comes to partnerships—we want to work with people that feel like family, that are trustworthy, and hold integrity high. My company is currently made up of my husband of twelve years, Christopher Murray, and my first college roommate, Heather Panzitta (who is now Coastal Kapital's head of funding) and others that have now become family.

Not only is my work rewarding, but the biggest perk of all is being married to my best friend and true love. We have created a healthy and positive mindset at home and in the office, which is lined with respect for one another, trust, and honesty. Working with my partner has allowed us to strive for goals that keep us moving in the same direction, and doing so created a happy home life since we have like-minded thoughts on growth. When we do take downtime, we are able to reflect on the company and the partnerships that brought this dream to life.

— *KORTNEY*

PART II

PASSION LEADS TO PURPOSE

CHAPTER 5

WHAT YOU VALUE

HANALEI SWAN

—Fashion Designer, International Speaker, and Bestselling Author of
How to Be & Raise an Unstoppable *Kid*

I was born thirty-three days early because of my parents' misunderstanding of wealth.

My mom and dad had planned to provide me with the life they never had growing up—a beautiful house with an ocean view, hearing the waves crash every morning with the white sand as their front yard, expensive cars, and enough money set aside so I didn't have to worry like their families did.

Even with all of their hard work and preparation, two months before I was born my parents found out they were about to lose everything financially. The dream of creating the perfect life for me came crashing down like an avalanche, pushing everything back to square one. The investments that were supposed to set us up for life became the reason they had to declare bankruptcy. This was the same real estate project that was supposed to allow my mom to quit her job and work from home so that I never had to be placed in daycare. That dream was merely a mirage.

The stress and legal pressure my mom was experiencing took a toll on her body and was the reason why I came thirty-three days early into this world . . . At least, that's what she thought. After a year of legal disputes and more stress, my parents had to make a drastic decision that would change the course of our lives forever.

Instead of fighting the legal battles and rebuilding what they lost, my parents realized that the "perfect life" they were trying to build for me might not be so perfect. The realization that this storm unleashed into our lives was more of a blessing than a curse became truer over time. On November 25, 2008, they decided to sell everything we owned and leave it all behind. We left San Diego, California, with $12,872.62 to our name and a vision and vow to create a new life that was no longer built on materialism.

Wealth is often defined as a plentiful supply of particularly desirable things. So, with that definition in mind, wealth can subjectively be anything that holds value to a particular person. What I have found most valuable in my life has been creating irreplaceable memories and impactful experiences; that is what makes me wealthy.

In my first fifteen years of life, my family and I traveled the world; we visited and lived in six continents and over twenty-four countries, bouncing around from school to school and meeting new people with different backgrounds and beliefs along the way. Growing up traveling, I never placed a lot of value on material things because I usually had to give away all my belongings every time we moved. I could only fit the most important things into my one, small suitcase. This is what made me realize the most important things I had in life weren't what I kept in my suitcase, but what I stored in my heart. My memories—the one thing other than family that is irreplaceable, the one thing I could never let go of.

"Someday this moment will fade away; the seconds we are living now will become only a memory to us. When we toil in the future or the past, we forget about the present and waste the only seconds on this earth we are truly guaranteed: the moments we are living now."—Hanalei Swan

DAD'S MEMORIES

I was always fascinated with reminiscing, spending so much time with my dad and asking him repeatedly to tell me a new surf story or an interesting tidbit from when he was my age.

He had so many memories that would captivate me for hours on end. I always wanted to be like both of my parents: great storytellers. Those moments together—watching the sunset with my dad and listening to him until dark—made me want to one day have worthy and exciting stories in my life to pass down to others. The stories of my mom and dad's past have already taught me so much, especially my dad's story.

He always starts it off with, "We never know when our expiration date may be."

My dad knew from a young age that his father was sick. When he was six years old, his mother and father got divorced and my dad found out his father was gay. The sickness my grandfather had was AIDS. He went from a hardworking entrepreneur to someone who had come to realize he now had a set expiration date. The doctors told him he would probably have less than a year to live. A switch flipped inside of his mind, his dream to see the world confronting him face-to-face. Because there was no guaranteed tomorrow, and he only had one life to live, he decided to start actually living again. Shortly after his diagnosis, he asked my dad at the age of twelve to fly to Europe with him to explore Amsterdam and England. This was the first flight in my dad's life.

My grandfather ended up beating the doctor's expectations and went on to live for five more years. In those years, my grandfather took my dad, uncle, and aunt across the world, creating once-in-a-lifetime experiences and showing them a completely new perspective compared to their farm-town life of less than two thousand people sitting just outside of Chicago. The family got to not only watch their father live out his bucket list but experience it with him too.

My grandfather passed away when my dad was sixteen. Even though I never got to meet him, my grandfather has had such a huge impact on my life. My dad being able to pass down his stories not only brought me closer to the grandfather I never knew but also taught me the importance of appreciating every day like it could be your last. That lesson has greatly impacted my life and how I see the world, making me appreciate all of the moments I've gotten to share with my dad and family, even the smallest ones. When you start to appreciate and show gratitude for what you have now, instead of dwelling on what you lack, you begin to surround yourself with abundance and fulfillment, and find beauty in the mundane.

In our lowest times, when we lost everything financially, the unspoken lesson of "never knowing when our expiration date may be" inspired my dad, twenty-five years later, to leave everything behind and travel the world again with our family. My dad passed down similar experiences to what his father gave him.

CAPTURING THE SMALL MOMENTS

I realized I wanted to live life by accumulating experiences instead of possessions while hiking up to Delicate Arch, at Arches National Park in Grand County, Utah. It is remarkable watching the sun dance against the delicately sculpted, bright orange rocks—the undulating surfaces morphed by water fifteen million years ago . . . It truly is a miraculous, otherworldly place.

Every time I revisit, I feel the same way as when I first hiked the arches. I drop into a complete feeling of bliss and presence, the rest of the world falls away, nothing else matters except the moment I'm living right then. Those trips have created some of my favorite memories with my family and deepened my appreciation for Mother Earth. I'd choose this memory over any material possession.

I've become a more present person from the travel experiences I have accumulated. These reflections make me value every moment that I get to experience. I look at each place as a new memory, and I get to choose how to remember it, realizing I have the ability to choose how I want to spend my time and create each moment of my life.

EVERYTHING STITCHED TOGETHER

When I was seven years old walking alongside my mom on the beach during sunset, she asked me, "What do you want to be now?" instead of the usual, "What do you want to be when you grow up?" My mom's spin on this question single-handedly opened my eyes to what I could truly do and be now!

At the time I didn't realize it, but she had planted a seed in my mind. I would go on to ponder a few years later, *If I could do anything now, what would it be?* School bored me like most kids my age, and I remember daydreaming to pass the time. *I could be an artist! Or maybe a photographer, or even a fashion designer!* A belief was instilled in me that if I put my mind to it, I could do anything. What if I actually took action on the thoughts that were always "just dreams"? The seed started to grow, and my parents helped me realize the importance of doing what you love and dedicating your time to doing what makes you happy. Through these experiences in my earlier years, I've been able to grow so much as a person, learning to be more open-minded and empowered to follow my heart, which led me to take the first steps to create my first company.

When I was eleven years old I started my first company making eco-friendly fashion. Thankfully, I had parents who wanted to support my dreams, empowering me to focus on what made me happiest in life. Growing up in a constantly changing environment, having open-minded conversations, and surrounding myself with people from different backgrounds, I found that what brought me the most joy in life was creating artwork and designing clothing. These experiences helped me become more open to exploring possibilities—especially in art and design—that I may not have if it weren't for my flourishing, everchanging environment and the people I met along the way.

HIGHEST VALUES

Your memories and experiences can help you find your highest values, and that can be your internal compass and guide for being wealthy in life. Through following my heart and trusting my intuition, I have been able to make the life I love.

I went to visit India with my dad, staying with locals an hour outside of Mumbai, for a giving-back trip with a company called Nalu. We donated over five hundred school uniforms to children who would otherwise have to leave school. It's one thing to read about poverty and the effect that pollution has on our planet, but it's another to live it and see it firsthand. Being there, watching rivers flow with bright colors from dying plants for fabric and trash being burned for heat, made me really take into question what I truly valued. I realized that the fashion industry, something I was passionate about, was actually harming our planet more than I knew. This humbling experience opened my eyes to the different possibilities of fashion, specifically using sustainable materials like bamboo and modal, as well as treating and paying our employees like humans, not machines. Without my trip to India, my values around the environment may not have developed into what they are today.

FINDING YOUR MATCH

Aside from using my experiences as a guide to help shape my values, something else that helped me figure out what I really love to do was writing down what gives me the most joy in my life and my vision for the future. Making me think about what I want to do, accomplish, and see. I let my pen carry me away through my mind, mapping my vision and my perfect day, converting those daydreams into affirmations and goals, picturing myself living in that future reality.

When you set visionary intentions for the future, it empowers you to continue carrying on, even if you lose sight or derail slightly. It is crucial to have your "why": the reason you are doing what you are doing. Think of it like a match by your side when you start to feel your fire fizzle out. Keep your vision with you and let it carry you to where you need to go. You are the writer of your own story; you get to choose what reality you want to live, experiences you want to make, and goals you want to accomplish.

IT'S NEVER TOO LATE TO START LIVING

Every day we are presented with the choice of how we want to spend that day, to choose how we want to feel and what we want to experience. Use your time wisely, don't let your bucket list stay a bucket list; it is never too late to start living.

What brings us the most wealth in our life isn't the money we have in the bank or the house we own. Your wealth comes from the experiences we live through and the memories we make.

The wealthiest and happiest people who left the most impact on me were never the richest ones in the room; they were the people who had stories to tell, converting their life experiences into wealth.

No matter who you are, you have the choice to do what makes you happy and change the life you live into the life you've dreamed of. All it takes is the first step, the first dream, goal, intention, and execution.

Remember to stay present and use the time you have to the fullest. These moments will one day become memories, so you might as well make them worth remembering.

— *HANALEI*

CHAPTER 6

FROM A VISION TO A CALLING

MICHALE GABRIEL

—Founder and CEO of Story by Design

I was thirty-six, in my backyard, eyes closed, and deep in meditation. Suddenly, in my mind's eye, appeared a globe of the world resting on a pair of hands. The words overhead were, "Peace through story." My heart started pounding. I could feel the words explode inside my head. Somehow, I knew I was being called to create peace in the world though storytelling. I had absolutely no idea what that would look like.

The week prior, I had attended a personal growth seminar that shook me to the core. I came home on a Friday night and consumed an entire bottle of wine by myself, which was totally out of character. On Saturday, I picked a fight with my husband. On Sunday, I started crying. I cried uncontrollably for a week. I knew something had happened to me; something had broken through, enabling me to experience parts of myself that I didn't even know existed. I was beginning to see who I was beyond the masks, my carefully crafted persona, and the story I had created to fulfill societal expectations. So when that vision came, I was ready to act on it.

I didn't know it then, but saying yes to that calling would become the source of my spiritual, emotional, and material wealth.

POWER OF STORY

I had used storytelling as a tool of connection before in major fundraising campaigns for non-profits and with children in a public

45

library setting, but this moment was different. This was a directive from my soul: I was to use story as a way to bring people to a place of peace within themselves and, thus, create more peace in the world.

I knew immediately that to fulfill this calling, I had to quit my job as Director of Development for the School of International Studies at the University of Washington and do it full-time—become an entrepreneur, start my own business, be recognized and paid for my ability to both tell stories and teach others to do the same.

With no real plan or strategy, I committed myself to doing just that.

My spouse and I had made decisions based on two incomes. He was not pleased that I was choosing to become self-employed. Every day when I'd come home, I would find him standing at the front door, asking me how much money I'd made. He wasn't the only one—another family member advised me to get a "real job," as if what I was being called to do wasn't real.

I soon realized that being a full-time, professional storyteller was not a financially stable situation. Yet, somehow, I knew that if I did this part-time, my calling would not be fully realized. I needed to trust that I would find a way. And later, when I was faced with choosing between my marriage or growing my vision, I chose my vision.

GROWING PAST FEAR

In the early years—especially after my divorce—I would look at my calendar, add up the revenue from scheduled storytelling bookings, and become overwhelmed with fear that I wouldn't be able to pay my bills. Sometimes I would lie in the fetal position, unable to get out of bed.

Amazingly, it was during those times I experienced the power of story to help me push past my own limiting beliefs, my own fear. That breakthrough has threaded its way into the storytelling coaching I do today. I needed a story big enough and bold enough to get me in an upright position to take action. I created one that not only included me but also every person called to express their gifts in service of a better world. I was taking action on behalf of them as well as myself. That story worked, every time.

Through all these twists and turns of finding my way professionally and generating an income, I began to realize that my beliefs around being worthy of financial success were greatly impacted by my childhood. I grew up in a single-parent family in an environment that was emotionally toxic. My mother, brother, sister, and I were barely sustained by court-mandated child support and alimony begrudgingly provided by my father. I was the child charged with asking for additional support for the family; however, I often returned from those missions empty-handed, feeling both unworthy and shameful for having failed my family—especially my mother. I had every reason not to trust the universe to have my back or support me in my efforts. Yet when I did choose to trust, I began to discover that everything that truly mattered to me, every need that ever surfaced, was met by saying yes to my calling.

Although my decision to become a full-time storyteller had initially rocked my financial stability, I found that I grew in other ways: confidence in my purpose and in the knowledge that I was making a difference in the lives of others. A child I'd met in the former Soviet Union summed it up saying, "You have led me to the land of fairytales and left me there facing my own dreams and feelings. I am so much better for it."

HUMAN CONNECTION

When I began storytelling in schools and keynoting at conferences, I traveled to urban cities and rural areas across the United States. I'd sometimes spend a week in village schools in Alaska, sleeping on a piece of foam in a kindergarten classroom, sharing my love of literature with children and coaching them to become storytellers themselves. I chose my stories carefully, making sure they embodied themes worthy of staying in a child's consciousness: generosity, tolerance, compassion, forgiveness . . .

After every performance, children and adults alike shared with me their own stories after being ignited by hearing mine. And in that exchange, a meaningful human connection was made. I discovered my voice had become a tool for personal transformation.

I began to look at my life and my calling in a new way. Doing this work, I felt wealthy in purpose. I began to understand that my wealth was directly connected to my ability to deeply connect with people and nourish them, using storytelling as the vehicle to do so.

This realization inspired me to establish the Storytelling Residency program at Seattle Children's Hospital. I secured independent foundation funding and engaged with over 1,500 patients and families over a ten-month period. When five-year-old Alex (permanently paralyzed from the neck down due to a car accident) spoke his first complete sentence aided by a tube in his trachea, it was because he wanted to participate in the stories. In our months of working together, Alex insisted on retelling my stories to others. The day he decided to tell me an original story, I knew that he was on his way to finding his own voice and creating meaning for his life. He left the hospital months later with the realization he was not confined by a body that held him captive. Alex had started the journey of finding the answer to the question he once asked his mother, "Mommy, I was happy inside your tummy. Why was I born?" And I was the one privileged to help facilitate the start of that process for him.

But when the funding for the hospital project ended, as well as the possibility of securing more, I was convinced that no other work could ever take its place. I could not imagine any other iteration of Peace through Story that would be more meaningful.

And yet, an invitation came to deliver a keynote for the Boeing Company Good Neighbor Annual Campaign Kickoff Breakfast. The audience included the CEO and two hundred senior vice presidents. The result? A whole new way for me to connect—this time with a corporate audience. At the end of my emotionally driven presentation, I received a standing ovation and became known as, The Woman Who Makes Grown Men Cry. I was invited to work as a consultant to the company in both the US and India for what has now become twenty-six years. My role? To teach leaders, over ten thousand of them, how to communicate from the heart. And what I discovered in the process is that each person's story I've coached into being has left an indelible impression on my own heart. That's how it works—when we tell our deeper stories, we help heal each other.

SOURCE OF MY CALLING

When I was fifty, I got a call from the daughter of my third-grade teacher, Mrs. Phyllis Norton, asking if her mother could attend my storytelling performances in Anchorage. I was traveling to Anchorage for a week of school performances, workshops, and public concerts. She said her mother had just returned to Anchorage after living forty years in Bend, Oregon. I was thrilled and, I must say, just a little nervous. I had delivered multiple keynotes for over 1,500 people, given thousands of performances, and been featured on Soviet television reaching over 50 million viewers . . . but this was different. This was my beloved (and demanding) third-grade teacher. She was now in her eighties. I had not seen her in over forty years.

When I first saw her in the school library, I was shocked. My Mrs. Norton had black hair; this Mrs. Norton had white hair. As a child I looked up at her; now I was looking down at her. But when she opened her mouth and started to speak, no doubt about it—this was *my* Mrs. Norton.

While storytelling, I would periodically look over at her and was thrilled that she was just as engaged as the children. After the last performance, I went up to Mrs. Norton and out of my mouth came a little third-grade voice I didn't know I still had. "Mrs. Norton, how did I do?"

Oh my god, I thought. *I'm fifty years old and still want my teacher's approval.*

"Dear," she said, "you were just wonderful."

Music to my ears.

I took her to dinner that night. We sat in a corner booth I had purposely reserved. We talked about my family: my mother's struggle with depression, her volatility, and her dependency on me. "You were shouldering adult responsibilities at home, Michale," she said, "In my classroom, I just wanted you to be a child."

When we finished eating, I said, "Mrs. Norton"—she tried to get me to call her Phyliss, but it just didn't feel right!—"would you do something for me?"

"Yes, dear, anything," she replied.

"Would you read to me like you did in the third grade forty-two years ago?"

"I'd love to, but I don't have a book!"

I said, "Oh, Mrs. Norton, I do." I took out of my bag a copy of a book she had read to my class. It was *Charlotte's Web*.

"What part do you want me to read?" she asked.

"Any part you want."

She selected the passage where Wilber the pig is being taken to the county fair. As soon as she started reading, I started scooting, closer and closer and closer until I was sitting right next to my third-grade teacher. Shoulder to shoulder. Close enough to not just hear her, but to feel her too. Then I shut my eyes and let her voice wash over me.

My love of story was seeded by this woman who not only read to us every single day, but who also encouraged me to stand in front of the class and share my own stories—ice fishing for the first time, winning a sewing contest, building a fort above our sandbox. I remember how I felt in her class: safe, nurtured, connected, valued, recognized . . . Now at age fifty, she was making me feel the exact same way.

Mrs. Norton died at the age of 106; I last visited her when she was 103. When it came time for me to leave, Mrs. Norton had begun to tire and, with her hand resting in mine, she fell asleep. I looked at our hands intertwined, forever together. I picked up my phone and took a photo of our hands.

When I received word she had died, I sat for a long time just looking at that photo.

Is it any wonder that her former student, who had been so enriched by the healing power of story from her childhood, would become a storyteller, a keeper of magic, even to this day at age seventy-seven?

Is it no wonder that my vision of creating Peace through Story would become my calling?

There is a beautiful indigenous teaching that says, "Today is a good day to fly and a good day to die." I live by that. When I am fully expressing the gifts I've been given—telling stories, helping others to tell theirs, listening deeply—I know in my heart it is indeed a good day to fly and a good day to die, because I am living my purpose on this earth.

So my advice to you? Listen to your heart. Do what you love. Follow your calling. Do not be afraid of the struggles along the path—those are your moments of initiation. They'll give you the chance to strengthen your resolve and recommit. Remember to give yourself the gift of pivoting into uncharted waters that might feel foreign to your original vision. You may discover that your soul has a much larger story in mind for you.

I know that by following your path, you will count yourself wealthy knowing you've inspired and impacted the lives of others. This is your ultimate source of contribution.

— *MICHALE*

CHAPTER 7

A BEAUTIFUL LIFE

ADRIANA MONIQUE ALVAREZ

—CEO and Founder of AMA Publishing and Author of *How to Start a Six Figure Publishing Company* and *The Younger Self Letters*

I didn't set out to create wealth, nor did I dream about starting a business. My dream was to travel the world and volunteer. I wanted to visit the places long forgotten about and take care of orphans and widows. I wanted to find the beauty in all of life, even the difficult parts. I would go on epic journeys to fulfil my dreams and define what true wealth means to me.

I was born and raised in a rural farming community a long way from nowhere and where everyone knew me. I was "Vernon and Dyanna's daughter," and if someone didn't make that connection, all I had to do was to mention my grandparents. At a young age, I understood what money could provide even if I didn't see it from an adult perspective.

My grandpa had been a truck driver, miner, and flailing entrepreneur before he struck gold. He decided to start a lumber business in the late seventies, which became the cash cow he had been searching for. Within ten years, my young parents went from bouncing checks to building a new house. My bedroom had one wall with the softest pink tulip wallpaper and a bedspread to match. I had a big closet and an en suite bathroom. I was in heaven! I had an appreciation for the finer things in life. What I discovered in my childhood was how much money could reveal about people.

It didn't take long for the small town to become a glasshouse. In the fifth grade, my teacher announced we were going to have a Valentine's

Day party and card exchange. My mom took me to pick out cards, and I carefully wrote one out to every kid in my class. The next day, I was dressed up as I proudly walked into class with my box full of love notes. When it was Elaine's turn, she walked around the room and placed a white envelope on each desk. As she approached me, she said loud enough for the entire class to hear, "Your parents can buy you a valentine. They're rich enough!"

EARLY EMBARRASSMENT

I could feel my face turn red. That was the day I learned not everyone was going to be happy about my good fortune. The older I got, the more I wanted to leave my hometown. I began to withdraw in high school. Instead of going to parties, I was filling notebooks with the places I wanted to see. In my senior year, I graduated a semester early and nothing gave me more relief than no longer walking the halls of my high school.

Everyone expected me to go to college, get a degree, and marry the neighbor. I left the most beautiful nest a child could ask for only a few months after graduating. My heart ached with homesickness, but I knew it was time for me to fly.

I went to central Florida to attend a four-week boot camp that would teach me how to live off the grid, without electricity or plumbing. I was taught a crash course on how to grow a garden and raise and butcher animals. I learned how to figure it out no matter what circumstances I encountered. I am sure everyone thought this spoiled girl would fall flat on her face, but I absolutely loved it. I went to bed with the sun every night, and each day I fell in love with the animals I was taking care of. I made bread better than I ever thought I could.

One night as we were talking over dinner, one lady mentioned the Kosovo War and that the state-run orphanage needed a full-time volunteer; I was their person. Within a few months, I was packing my bags for Tirana, Albania.

DANCE, SWIM

I spent the summer with the kids on the Adriatic Sea. We slept in an abandoned building and ate cucumbers and tomatoes for breakfast.

The kids loved to swim all day and dance at night. The water was clear and calm, and I had never experienced this kind of raw beauty. I was in a whole new world, and I was literally living my teenage dream.

At the end of the summer, I returned to Colorado and made the decision to move to Tirana, Albania. I knew I would not be going to college, getting a degree, and applying for a high-paying, corporate job. I had no desire to enter the rat race and find each day exactly like the last. I wanted to take care of kids that had no one, and I wanted to show them their life could be beautiful. I flew out with eight duffle bags stuffed full of clothes, toiletries, and toys for 120 kids. My mom helped me get settled, and when it was time for her to go, I cried for days. It was my turn to give back and to be the rock my parents had always been for me.

QUESTIONS, DESPAIR

Most of the kids didn't have either parent or some had been separated from their siblings. One night, I buried my head in my pillow and I said, "What am I doing here? I have no formal training to help these kids with the pain they have been through. I cannot save them. I cannot go back and change their past. I cannot lift the sadness of this country for all it has been through. What can I actually *do* for them?"

That is when I heard the still, small voice that would become my Guide for Life. It said, "No, you cannot save them or fix the bigger issues this country or these children are facing. What you can do is create small moments of joy with them. What you can do is love them. What you must do is look for the beauty in each moment."

That became my only focus, my full-time job. One day, I found a little old man selling popcorn in the city center. I walked the kids down, and we had a great time playing and eating popcorn. For Christmas, I threw them a party and we danced all night. When they got hurt, I hugged them. When they laughed, I laughed with them.

DEFINING MY LIFE

After three years, I went on to do the same at an HIV-baby orphanage in Nairobi, Kenya. I would take the babies outside to play in the sunshine and hold them one at a time until they fell asleep for their nap. I could hear Bob Marley playing in the distance, and I made simple moments of connection my highest priority.

I returned to the United States after contracting the deadliest strain of malaria, but it turned out to be a blessing. That was the year I met my husband, Derek, on a blind date and quickly became engaged to be married. I asked him for one thing: that we create a beautiful life. I told him I didn't want him to have a good job or make lots of money if it meant leaving our home for eight, ten, or even twelve hours a day. I told him I'd rather live in our car than become the kind of people who didn't share meals around the table.

We started a business together in 2009 and have worked together every day since. We never made money our number one goal; we have always come back to creating a life we love. When we added babies to the mix and our family grew, this became even more important. Nothing asked me to get my priorities straight like the loving faces of my two boys. I could feel them watching our every move, and more importantly, I could feel the influence we had in their lives. If these boys became us, would that be a good or bad thing?

Derek and I took them to see the world right after they were born. We worked a few days a week and filled most of our time with adventures most only dream of. They have played in Frida Kahlo's courtyard, cheered at the Day of the Dead parade in Mexico City, chased the waves in Costa Rica, stuffed themselves with Greek yogurt and honey, celebrated Easter at the Vatican, spent the summer at Lake Como, felt like kings in Dubrovnik, ran around the monasteries of Montenegro, and spent countless summer days in the gentle waters of the Adriatic Sea.

We expanded in 2019 by adding a publishing division to our business. When the world changed in 2020, I spent three months grieving my sense of freedom. Being locked in a house wasn't my idea of living. I knew we wouldn't have to follow any of these rules in my small hometown. There we could be near family, and my kids could have a happy childhood picking raspberries in the mountains, making s'mores in the backyard, and chasing their dogs around the yard.

RIPENING

We drove four days out of the Yucatan to Colorado, and when we pulled into my grandparent's driveway, I knew without a shadow of a doubt we were home. The piano my Papa C.R. gave me was in the living room. Derek's art was on the walls. The same fridge I used to get snacks from was still in the kitchen. We now work a few days and spend the rest renovating the house and property: check on the plums and peaches to see if they are ripe yet, plant hundreds of tulips and daffodils for spring, fill the pantry with healthy food, add to the orchard, plan the greenhouse, put ladybugs in the herbs garden . . .

When the world doesn't make sense and my heart feels heavy, I remember what I heard in that cold, concrete room in the orphanage. While I can't fix the bigger issues of our world, and I can't save us from what is unfolding, I can create moments of joy. I can make chocolate soufflé for breakfast. I can color with the boys and pray for them at bedtime. I can let Derek hold me on the couch. I can invite my parents over for dinner.

A RICH, BEAUTIFUL LIFE

A beautiful life has always been synonymous with a wealthy life for me. Society would love to sell us all on something that looks like going into debt for higher education, climbing corporate ladders while selling our souls, and filling our homes with stuff that we don't have time to enjoy. It is our job to ask, "Is this what I always dreamt of? Is this what lasts? And what will matter when I'm eighty-eight years old looking back over my life?"

What about you? What fills your heart with joy?

NO VALIDATION

I want to live in a world that values health, relationships, and watching the sun set with a grateful heart—this is true wealth in my book.

How can you create a beautiful life? It starts with defining what that looks like for you. Most of us do not even know what we want our life to look like because we are simply following the plan our parents, educators, or religious leaders had for our lives. I found taking time away from it all helps quiet the voices around me. Taking even twenty-four hours to be in nature, far from cell towers and Wi-Fi, creates tremendous clarity.

The next step is looking at how to incorporate what is important to you into your everyday life. For example, every day I look at my schedule in the morning and carve out a chunk of time to do something fun with my boys. Some days we eat watermelon together and talk about baseball; other days we go to the farmer's market or go swim in the river. It doesn't matter what it is as long as it's quality time together.

Taking time for self-reflection on a regular basis also helps ensure that I stay on track. I take at least two days off each week and one week of each month. That might sound like more than you can take, but if you start with looking at your calendar and blocking off time to rest, play, and connect with yourself, it goes a long way to creating a beautiful life.

Last but not least, I have found it's not easy for overachievers to know when they have arrived. Most people want more money no matter how much they have made. They want more accomplishments, and success becomes a drug as addictive as any. What I recommend is pausing for celebration often and before setting another goal.

May you find the courage to stop and ask yourself, "What does a beautiful life mean to me?" It is there you will find true wealth.

—*ADRIANA*

CHAPTER 8

ABUNDANT LIVING

DANA KAY

—CEO and Founder of the ADHD Thrive Institute and
Board-Certified Holistic Health and Nutrition Practitioner

My life was a mess. I knew it. My husband knew it. And on this particular day, everyone at Costco in Seattle, Washington, knew it too.

"But I don't want to wait!" My eldest son, Oliver, held a box of crackers in his hands, trying to open the top before I could snatch it away. We were in the freezer aisle, and I was almost finished with my grocery list. I could see the exit doors right ahead. So close.

"Just a little bit longer," I told him. "We're almost done. Once we've paid for them, you can have as many as you want." I hoped—naively—that this promise would hold him over. But deep down, I knew what was coming next. This wasn't my first rodeo.

Oliver threw himself onto the supermarket floor.

"I want it now!" he screamed, flailing his limbs like a completely out-of-control octopus. I watched in horror as his legs neared a spaghetti sauce endcap. One foot hit a jar of sauce and sent it flying onto the floor. Glass shattered. Sauce splattered everywhere. My face grew hot and turned red from embarrassment.

That's when I heard a comment from a young, pregnant woman in high heels standing a few feet away. "I'm never going to let my kid do *that*," she whispered to her friend standing beside her. They both shook their heads and then looked away.

You might be wondering why I'm sharing such an embarrassing story. I'm sharing it because I imagine you've had days like this too, days when you wished you could disappear.

My big wish that day was to escape my life. Have you ever felt like this? Have you ever wanted to run away from your life?

On that day, I didn't want to deal with my son's tantrums anymore. I didn't want to walk on eggshells, waiting for the next meltdown. I didn't want to feel judged every time we left the house because of my son's behavior.

I wanted happiness. Peace. Joy. Wealth.

Not monetary wealth—though, of course that would be nice too. More than that, I wanted abundant-life wealth. I wanted to actually enjoy my day-to-day life, delight in my family, and find meaning in my work. Since you're reading this book, you probably want some of these things too, but maybe you think they're too far out of reach. I also felt that way back then.

That night, I went home and told my husband, Ben, "Honestly, I don't even like my own child."

Of course I loved him, but I didn't *like* him—not when his behavior was so challenging. Still, what kind of mother actually says those words out loud?

Something had to change, but I never expected our entire lives to be turned upside down.

The next day, I made a phone call to my son's doctor. Shortly after that, we went in for an evaluation, and Ollie was diagnosed with attention deficit hyperactivity disorder (ADHD). His doctor handed me a prescription and sent us on our way. He didn't tell us about any other options besides medicine, so I did what any other parent in my situation would likely do: I listened to his advice.

When Oliver had side effects from that medication, and the doctor suggested adding a second and then a third, I listened again. He was the expert, after all. Who was I to suggest anything different from what the expert was saying?

I'll tell you who. I'm Oliver's *mom*. I'm the person who probably knows him better than anyone else. I should have listened to my gut when those medications weren't working for him. I should have trusted myself more than I trusted someone else.

When that same doctor suggested the fourth medication for my young son—exclusively to manage side effects caused by the other three—I finally stopped listening to him and started listening to the voice inside telling me enough was enough.

Have you ever heard that inner voice telling you what to do next? Maybe you've spent years hushing it, forcing it to quiet down, and assuming it didn't know what was best for you. When I finally started listening to my inner voice, my entire life's trajectory changed.

ONE DECISION THAT CHANGED EVERYTHING

I started looking into alternative ADHD treatments that didn't require multiple prescriptions with side effects we couldn't ignore. I learned about the gut-brain connection.

The foods we eat can affect every area of our lives: from emotional regulation, mood, and behavior to ADHD symptoms and a host of other areas that might not seem to be related to food but are. Food is powerful, and the more I learned, the more I changed our family's diet.

Slowly, my son's behavior began to change. We stopped dreading each day and began to enjoy our time together. We got off the emotional rollercoaster we'd been on for years. Tantrums used to be daily but were happening less and less.

As I continued to adjust our diet—getting rid of inflammatory foods like gluten, dairy, and soy, and providing nutrient-dense, whole foods like fruits and vegetables, healthy fats, and grass-fed animal protein— symptoms that used to wear down our entire family began to fall by the wayside. My son's ADHD symptoms stopped controlling him, and he became the child I always knew he could be.

When Oliver was first diagnosed with ADHD, I worked in business and accounting. I assumed that's where I would stay. But the more I learned about the effects of food on children with ADHD and other similar disorders, the more I felt pulled in another direction.

You might feel pulled in another direction too. It can be hard to change. I've been there.

But after witnessing the transforming power of food with my own eyes, how could I not share this information with others?

I had to.

I went back to school and became a board-certified holistic health and nutrition practitioner, opened a practice, and began helping other caregivers of children with ADHD. What I have realized since then is that this career change has also played a large part in the abundant life I have now. I enjoyed my work before, but I am passionate about my work now. Helping other caregivers find the same peace and joy that my family has found has given my life meaning and purpose, or in other words . . . wealth. I love reassuring caregivers that they have options to help their children outside of medication.

Medication isn't bad and has its place, but it's not always the right solution for every child.

Today, so much of the medical world takes a cookie-cutter approach: if a patient has X, they get Y. There's very little personalization involved.

Parents need to know they have options besides a prescription. If a medication causes side effects, or if a family does not want to go down that pharmaceutical route, there are alternatives that are just as effective—and at times, even more effective. It's possible to find relief from ADHD symptoms without popping a pill. Parents need to know this information, and I decided I would be one of the people to tell them.

Over time, that decision led to a ripple effect. What started as just one person has now grown and spread. As more people learn, they teach those around them, expanding the ripple exponentially.

I don't dread my day-to-day life anymore. Not only are my son's ADHD symptoms better, thus giving our household a sense of peace and calm, but I'm also doing work that I love, not just clocking in for a paycheck.

Do you dread your life? Do you wish your family was different? Do you wish you were doing something you felt more passion for? I've been there, and I know how hard that can be. I also know it doesn't have to stay that way.

In fact, I'm now living that abundant life I always thought was out of reach, in large part because my son's ADHD symptoms are gone. He isn't on any medications and is doing better without them than he ever did with them.

But there's another reason I'm living the abundant life, something that has nothing to do with my son's behavior and everything to do with my career. Now, I'm not working solely for a paycheck; I'm working in my passion and helping other families do the same. I'm living the life I was meant to live.

You might not be able to imagine living a life of passion, enjoying each day, and looking forward to the future, but it's possible for you too.

KEYS TO ABUNDANT LIVING

That grocery store trip turned out to be the best thing that ever happened to me, because it was the triggering event that led to everything I'm doing now.

I don't know why you picked up this book on wild, wealthy living, but I do know this: you picked it up because you were meant to read it.

Something inside you needed you to read the stories within the pages of this book. Maybe you picked it up because you want to live an abundant life too. Maybe you're wondering how that's even possible based on your current circumstances. Looking at life today, maybe you can't imagine it ever being any different, any better. I want you to know it can be.

Abundant living isn't nearly as far off as it might seem. It all begins by doing the following three things:

Key One: Listen to the Right People

More than anything else, listening to the right people means listening to *yourself*, trusting your instincts, and quieting the inner critic that says you're wrong. It means doing extensive research on something, then trusting that research and your own gut instinct instead of blindly doing something just because someone else says it's what you should do. It means that if someone tells you to do something you don't think is the right thing, you don't have to listen to them. Certainly, there is value in gathering wisdom from others, but *not* if it means ignoring your own intuition.

You might have been told you wasted your life. I know I wasted months of my life battling side effects caused by medication that I knew in my gut was not what my son needed. That's not to say medication is not right for you or your family. You must trust *your* gut and whatever it is telling you. My only regret is not listening to my instincts sooner. I hope you'll listen to yours.

Living an abundant life begins by listening to yourself!

Key Two: Find Your Passion

When I was working in business and accounting, I worked for a paycheck. I enjoyed things about my job and the people who worked there, but it wasn't my passion. It was a means to an end. I was making a living but not enjoying life.

If you're not loving what you're doing, then maybe you shouldn't be doing it. Find your passion. Live your dream life. Don't settle for just making a paycheck. Life is more than money, and wealth is more than having cash in a bank account. True wealth is living your dream life; it's in abundance, in passion, in joy.

Key Three: Share Your Passion

I get so much joy from helping other families find the same freedom from ADHD symptoms that my family has found. One of the children we worked with used to eat only five total foods, but now he eats more than one hundred. He used to have daily rage episodes, but those are nonexistent now that his family has changed how they eat.

Another child used to get in trouble constantly at school. One year, he and his brother had thirty-seven total suspensions. The next year, once his mom learned the powerful effects of food and changed their diets, these children had zero suspensions. In fact, they even won awards at school for their good behavior.

Helping these people didn't only help them . . . it also blessed me!

When we give to others out of our passion, we are blessed in return. The universe, a higher power, or God—whatever you believe in—does not give us gifts so that we can hoard them for ourselves but so that we can share them for the greater good.

If you want to live an abundant life, listen to the voice that matters most: yours. Find your passion, then share that passion with the world around you. Our gifts are meant to be shared with those around us, and *that*, my friends, is when abundant living really begins.

—Dana

PART III

MIND, BODY, AND SPIRIT WEALTH

CHAPTER 9

THE NATURE OF ABUNDANCE

CAMBERLY GILMARTIN

—Senior Marketing Communications Strategist and
Project Manager for Curious Ant Creative

For me, health is wealth. I believe that the ability to connect to oneself—to quiet the rush of continual thinking and unite with our own calm, steady heart and the vastness of all—is more precious than gold. I do my best work, am able to create at my fullest, and achieve at my optimum potential when I am of sound mind. This is why, for me, health is the very essence of wealth and abundance. When connected, I move acutely from an inner calm with awareness of my feelings and emotions as well as an understanding of how my words and actions impact or inspire others. Consciously creating stillness every day for the close observation of, and connection to, myself and nature allows me to deeply listen and respond intentionally from my heart. For me, inner stillness, when prioritized consistently, creates a state of continual positive mental and physical health—the essence of true abundance. I am grateful to have discovered early on the immense value of slowing down and intentional cultivating stillness in each day.

A FORCE GREATER THAN MYSELF

I've heard it said that we are born connected to our hearts, then we grow up and spend the rest of our lives figuring out how to reconnect with that place within ourselves. As a child, I tuned in from a place of feeling, which I experienced most strongly in nature—especially in forests, at the tops of high mountains, and near water. I sensed the presence of and felt deeply connected to a force much greater than myself. There, a flow of information, questions, and answers continually sprung forth; I intuitively trusted these.

Over the years, I began to consciously understand that what I was experiencing was a connection to my Divine Essence. I use the term Divine Essence to encapsulate the concept of spirit. When connected, I became aware that I was united with the Divine Essence of all people and things all at once. Later, I discovered that it was possible to tap into this to seek answers, ask for aid, serve humanity, and create wealth in my life.

By making stillness a part of each day, we create the opportunity to connect to our essence and the abundant essence of all. Every one of us has this powerful ability. Connecting to our essence doesn't have to mean taking a trip to the mountains or ocean (though, in my experience, simply being in nature can allow for effortless connection). It is also entirely possible to connect indoors, in crowded areas, or pretty much anywhere. As I learned from Savitri, my spiritual mentor, we must simply breathe, think of a beautiful feeling, and then stay with it! The emphasis here is on feeling. It's important to deeply connect to a moment in your life when you felt joy. I often use a memory of my daughter as a baby during a trip to the sea. I think about how I held her wriggly body on my hip and waded out waist-deep into the water. She and I bounced up and down together in the waves as I sang her a funny made-up song about us. Everything about that moment fills me with pure joy: her giggly baby face and wide eyes taking it all in, the sparkling blue waves and feeling of saltwater prickling against my skin, the sunset, the ocean smells, and the sounds of her laughter. In that moment, I felt deeply, universally connected, filled with peace and love. I hope this memory can help you recall one of your own to tune into and feel.

HEALTH FROM THE OUTSIDE, IN

During the summer before I was to start high school, my parents moved us from a small town in Minnesota to the Pacific Northwest. It was a tough adjustment for a soft-spoken tomboy who rode her ten-speed to school and spent more time inside books than studying fashion or makeup; however, I eventually managed to find my place. Thankfully, the shimmering Emerald City of Seattle offered plenty of nature—water, trees, and mountains—allowing me to continually connect with my Divine Essence.

Nature has always been a safe haven for me. To be able to hear, feel, and connect in stillness to my Divine Essence, I intuitively knew that I needed to be silent in and with nature. At the same time, experiencing this connection has allowed me to both feel and understand at a very deep level that I am enough, that I do not need anything else to feel the highest high and deepest love imaginable. This truth exists for every single one of us everywhere when we learn how to tune in!

During high school, I began to hone my love for writing, and the practice of yoga and meditation also entered my life. Immediately, the yogic teachings felt like old friends, and the knowledge and regular practice of yoga and meditation were a tremendous relief during the turbulent teen years when I, like many young people, sought to understand my true self. In yoga and meditation, I found the familiar stillness and connection to my Divine Essence. These practices provided a similar solace from the feelings of uncertainty about who I was and where I fit in to life that being out in nature did for me. I have always enjoyed sports, animals, and being outdoors, so I paid close attention to health and maintaining a physically strong body and clear mind.

DISCOVERING ABUNDANCE

When was the last time you sat silently in the beauty of nature and allowed your heart to be filled with its abundance, given yourself a few minutes to write your feelings, or quietly held your favorite yoga pose? The stillness and abundance that is felt and experienced in these activities exists within you. When we connect to our Divine Essence, we tune into infinite wealth and opportunity, into the Divine Essence of all. This Divine Essence is creation energy and exists within each one of us. It is with creation energy that our unique gifts are able to come out of us and into the world—whatever form they may be. These unique gifts are the riches, wealth, and abundance that we have inside of us to share with the world from our heart and perspective. We are all one. There is no separation. Where one is suffering pain and sorrow, the whole suffers. The reverse is also true: where one is experiencing deep joy and love, the entire universe benefits.

Life requires patience and courage because the answers are not always shown at once. I have experienced my fair share of heartbreak, pain, and sadness. Through these more difficult experiences, the biggest being a divorce from the father of my children whom I deeply loved, I learned that we always have the choice to immediately connect with our Divine Essence instead of the pain.

I often explain the insight I gained from my divorce as the tearing up of my Norman Rockwell painting. You likely can imagine the scene: a perfectly coiffed couple around an immaculately set table with smiling, well-dressed children, an obedient dog at their side—and let's not forget a white picket fence! I needed to mourn this ideal vision as I set out on my journey as a divorced single mom.

Over the last few years, I've gotten divorced, worked a full-time job, started a company, sold my house, moved my two children and myself in with my aging parents, started and finished an MBA program, assisted my ninety-year-old friend in the completion of her memoir, helped to launch a community nonprofit, raised (at times turbulently) my two teens during a global pandemic, and more. There were many days when I wondered how I would manage to survive the hour, much less the week. I tell you this because I want everyone reading this who may be doubting me to understand that if I could do all this (and more), then so can you! The beautiful thing is it all becomes easier when you are consistently creating stillness and connecting to your Divine Essence! Abundance is awaiting your arrival in your heart.

DOING YOUR DIVINE

Living a life of connection takes patience, courage, and a willingness to spend time in stillness and nature—which is *so* worth it! Ultimately life itself is a beautiful, crooked line . . . and that's okay. We are exactly where we are meant to be right now. The ability to connect into our Divine Essence when making decisions or seeking answers allows us to tune into our heart . . . and the heart is never wrong. Hardship and difficulty are meant to inform, teach, help us connect even more closely, and *then* refine. With every insight and further refinement comes the opportunity to experience greater health, wealth, overall abundance, and deeper joy and connection in every area of our lives. By intentionally creating time to consistently connect every day, I developed the ability to deeply listen, better discern, and see more vividly. These abilities enhanced my overall awareness. I began to notice, pay attention to, and take action on the many signs and clues provided on my journey directing me toward the people, projects and experiences best aligned with my higher purpose and greatest potential. In hindsight, it's clear that if I had not made time for stillness and practiced tapping into and connecting with my Divine Essence on a consistent basis, I very well could have chalked the universe's subtle signs and messages up as meaningful coincidence or synchronicity.

As I have continued to intentionally connect with and live from my Divine Essence, it has informed me about every project I involve myself with or agree to work on. Within the last three years, it's become clear that everything I work on I am meant to be doing, and that each one is connected to my greater purpose, for the good of all.

Following my divorce, I had a serendipitous encounter with two friends and ended up working with tBUG. A global community garden, tBUG shares a dream of universal importance: that the food we eat is inseparable from the land and conditions in which it is grown. Healthy food is the root of healthy kids, families, community, wellness, and connection. There it is again—the connection of health to wealth and abundance! Today, I am coauthoring this amazing book. As a result, I've also coauthored a chapter in another collaborative book project.

My decision to involve myself in each of these projects came out of intentionally creating stillness as well as connecting to my own Divine Essence and that of all. From stillness and connection, I was able to truly hear and feel the unified mission of abundance, unity, and shared wealth that all of these projects share. When our work is aligned with our heart, it becomes joyful. When we are connected to ourselves, we are able to tune in and notice when things we are doing are out of alignment. The next time you find yourself feeling disconnected, confused, or have a difficult decision to make, I invite you to create stillness—in nature, whenever possible. Then from there, connect to your Divine Essence. Quietly tune into your heart and deeply listen. Ask yourself what is bubbling up there for you, and the answers will come. Are you struggling with a loved one? Unable to find time to spend where you want to? Feeling helpless, disillusioned, or ill? For me, the answers that arose meant taking action to pivot the type of work I was doing so I could better support my children, selling my home to be closer to family, forging new relationships, and reprioritizing fitness and nutrition. By creating space and time for calmness and connection, I was able to see and take the necessary actions that shifted myself and my family into abundance—physically, mentally, and financially.

MORE THAN ENOUGH

My desire for each of you reading this is that you will consciously take time to slow down, create stillness, and connect with your Divine Essence. When you connect to this place within yourself, with nature, you may experience a connection to the universal Divine Essence. You may realize that you are one with nature, just as we are all one with one another. In nature, abundance is absolutely evident. Look at a field of flowers or a billion blades of grass, the vastness of the sky, endless stars, or countless raindrops. In nature, there are innumerable colors, patterns, and textures, infinite species and scents. Abundance is visible everywhere in nature. When we connect and become one with this energy, we open up an infinite flow of abundance and wealth. It is from this place that it becomes possible to clearly understand that you, exactly as you are, are enough. Connecting to our Divine Essence is connecting to creation energy, and it is here that we realize our fullest potential. We do our best work, create at our fullest, achieve our optimum potential when we are of sound mind. Consciously creating stillness every day for the close observation of, and connection to, ourselves and nature allows us to deeply listen and respond from our own heart. Taking the time to slow down and create stillness is a conscious, positive health choice. Inner stillness, when prioritized consistently, creates a state of continual positive mental and physical health, which is for me the essence of true abundance.

— *CAMBERLY*

CHAPTER 10

YOUR MILLIONAIRE KARMA

STEFANIE BRUNS

—CEO of Business Flow Academy, Quantam Psychologist, and Business Mentor

When looking at wealth, we must view it with an awareness of the social programming aspect of money, richness, and prosperity. Wealth is a personal journey that is made up of several layers, starting from childhood and early teachings from our parents and teachers. While growing up, we learn from our environment what wealth means, and sometimes we even learn that it is a bad thing. So it is important to start now, with our very own definition of wealth. What does being wealthy mean to you? To me, wealth in our lives is about the reward of doing something meaningful and creating change in the lives of others. It also includes an abundance in all areas of life not only financially, but also on different levels. For example: living in a healthy body, having loving relationships with the people around me, and enjoying the life I desire.

It is important to dive a little deeper into why most people are not wealthy. As a quantum psychologist, I help people discover what blocks them from living their dream life filled with wealth on all levels. Looking from a holistic perspective, we see the influence of their ancestral line and the collective field. There are many layers of our early programming, which include the mental aspect, our thought systems, and even our DNA levels and genetics.

Every person has a special energetic blueprint (your state of being or your energy, also known as your soul-print) that is connected to their life experiences, which are complex and differ from person to person. Through testing, we find the root of the problem and release what I call the Millionaire Karma, which are the difficulties or challenges related to their connection to wealth. It is important to release the Millionaire Karma in order to tap into the field of financial abundance. All the blockages we have against being wealthy and abundant that we collected from our parents and grandparents, and even in former incarnations, is called the Millionaire Karma.

People that want to go into business sometimes make the mistake of not practicing a relationship with the energetic and healing aspect of themselves, which can relieve the blockages keeping them caged away from the quantum field. A connection to the quantum field will help you gain access to the universal wisdom and infinite possibilities, because it is the energy field that surrounds us and where all the data are stored on an energetic level.

ENERGETIC SIGNATURES

Today, as a quantum psychologist, I combine quantum physics, self-development healing, and psychology in my work. Quantum physics helps us to see human beings with a holistic approach as we get a deeper understanding of how our energy system is connected to the energy field of the whole universe. That way, we can use the universal laws of quantum physics, applying them to our daily life to reach our goals and dreams. On my own journey and in our work with thousands of clients of my company, Business Flow Academy, we focus on going deep into their own energetic blueprint and healing the blockages keeping them stuck (i.e., the Millionaire Karma). That way it becomes easy to scale the business and attract wealth.

Through energy healing, pineal gland detoxification, meditations, and quantum leap hypnosis, we guide people into their ideal state and timeline where the best version of themself (I call it Ideal Energetic Signature) lives the life of their dreams. In a state of theta brainwaves, we can easily delete all the old programs and blockages, thereby making space to download all the new skill sets, habits, and knowledge that their Ideal Energetic Signature already has. Clients describe undergoing massive shifts when we show them how to connect with their intuition and lead them to the direct door of the universal field of their own never-ending wisdom.

STORY OF BELIEF TO BRAVERY

Sometimes all you need to do is make a brave decision. For me, that moment happened in 2015. It was a rainy, dark, and cold autumn afternoon in Germany. I was at home with our two toddlers and a baby, reflecting on my life and realizing that my husband spent more time with his work colleagues than with us.

I thought, *We have studied for so long, two academics (psychologist and architect), but we still don't have enough money to spend more time together.*

I was a strong entrepreneur who never stopped working, even as a young mother with her children at home and not in daycare. When my husband got home, I started working; when he was on vacation, I held my retreats and workshops. We had three wonderful children at this time, two of them born without medical help. The third delivery was more complicated. I was brave enough to have my breech baby at home without the pressures of invasive medicine but not brave enough to live the life I wanted.

That nasty afternoon, I decided to make a change and create the wealth that I desired on all levels, including spending more quality time with my loved ones.

I thought, *It must be possible to be in a warmer country during the cold central European winter months.*

So three months later, we sold almost all our stuff and moved to Portugal. I promised my husband that I would cover the costs with my online business, although I had no idea how to do that at the time. We bought a totally overgrown plot of land and lived in a yurt for one year. We built a permaculture garden, a small house out of a ruin.

All of this sounds super romantic, but we had a big problem: my online business started well, but I couldn't scale it. After six months, we were left with no money or savings and no relatives or friends who could help. There was great suffering during this time, and we nearly resorted to selling our wedding rings in order to afford groceries. This was an emotional decision, but we kept them due to the low offer. The summer was full of fear of not having enough money to feed our kids. I invested the last money I had to get a business coach, but I could only afford the first installment and had no clue how to pay the rest of it. But what I knew was that it would work out in the end. For me, coaching was the only way to grow my business at that time so we could survive financially. Together with my business partner, we made it through this summer building up our coaching company, and when autumn came, we went to Germany where I had a speaker performance.

When I looked at my phone the next day, people texted me, "Are you still alive?" Our property got hit by a huge forest fire. Everything was gone, but my first thought was, *Okay, the fire can take our goods, the acre of forest, and our garden, but it cannot burn my knowledge.*

Shortly after we cut down all the burned trees, we needed a break, so we went to the beach. I took all my online office equipment with me because that's all I had to make money. When we returned to our car, we saw that a thief had stolen all my last resources!

But here, too, my first thought was, *Nobody can steal my knowledge.*

Three years later, there was an abrupt falling-out with my former business partner. On May 27, 2020, I lost the business that I had been building up with her for the last four years from one day to the other. Again, my first thought was that nobody could steal my knowledge, creativity, and unstoppable faith.

The only possibility of a bright future for my family and myself in Portugal was my connection to the energy field. When you have a connection to the field and the infinite wisdom of all that is, you know exactly what to do without a shadow of a doubt.

I developed my own business concept within twenty-four hours, started my online business from scratch, and taught myself how to create videos and set up programs. I worked eighty-to-ninety hours a week, and within a short time, I was generating six figures a month and had set up a multimillion-dollar business with my special approach to wealth creation, which I am now teaching to my clients. Today it is a multimillion-dollar business.

I'm sharing this with you to tell you that you can always improve your game. If a simple girl from central Germany can do it, you can too. No fire, no thief, and no treachery can stop you. There is literally nothing stopping you from improving your game.

REVOLUTIONIZED

I've been doing this kind of work for over seventeen years and have noticed quite an evolution in people becoming more open to inner work and healing. It is spoken about much more and has inspired an awakened community to explore their extrasensory perceptions. You may have heard of it; a lot of people talk about "The Great Awakening," a phase—hopefully in the near future—where we see all people in the world revolutionized by their inner wisdom. However, compared to the early 2000s, I see that we have evolved closer to that phase at a fantastic rate because more and more people take the time to work on themselves.

Everybody is connected to the quantum field, and when you find the link, you connect with your inner peace, joy, and love. Most people in business that have found the link to the field are usually spiritually connected but have yet to connect themselves to physical wealth gain. That's where the work on our Millionaire Karma is important— removing the energetic blockages that keep us from living a life filled with abundance. A good tip to start with that work is: analyze all the beliefs you have about money, and discover—perhaps in hypnosis— what kind of negative emotions you link with having a lot of money.

UNBLOCKING YOUR PROSPERITY

Prosperity is our birthright, and many people who come to me struggle with imposter syndrome or think they are undeserving of wealth in all areas of life. When we release those blockages, we can enter a new world of endless possibilities, inner freedom, and wealth—whether spiritual, monetary, or both.

As infinite beings, I don't believe we have limitations. There is no reason to choose between being more spiritual or more business oriented. We have the ability to heal and embody the cosmic mission that helps us to combine both.

How to unblock Millionaire Karma, so that you can access the spiritual and monetary alignment, get over that imposter syndrome, and find your cosmic mission:

1. Through kinesiologic muscle testing, we can easily find out if you have any Millionaire Karma. The chances are high if you haven't earned and kept millions yet. (By the way, even millionaires can suffer from Millionaire Karma if they have a fortune but don't live a fulfilled life. But don't worry—in both cases, we can easily burn Millionaire Karma.)

2. After we have determined if Millionaire Karma is blocking you, we can go through the process of burning it. There are several methods, such as breathing techniques, cord-cutting tools, or a fire ritual. What is very important to understand is: in all methods, we use our most powerful force, intention-setting.

3. There are thousands of karma-burning methods out there, but you need a facilitator that will precisely locate the root karma and delete it in all timelines and dimensions.

4. Once you've deleted your Millionaire Karma, you will feel that you are good enough and worthy to live a life in abundance. But the best part is that you will be free to ascend to higher levels of energies and, therefore, vibrate on the same level as your goals. From there on, it is only a question of time—in other words, when you will reach your goals and fulfill your cosmic mission.

JUICINESS OF LIFE

The proof that our systems are successfully working is not only the outstanding results of my clients but also my own experiences. After I had to restart my company from scratch in 2020, I created an empire that became widely known in the German self-development and business-coaching market in less than two years. Seeing the success of my clients makes me realize how blessed I am to live the life I truly desire and show people to do the same with ease and joy. If we can see the challenges that occur in our life as something helping us to grow and to step into our true power, we can be thankful for everything that happens for us. In the end, by staying consistent and never losing faith in ourselves, we will be able to enjoy the juiciness of a life filled with wealth on all levels.

COSMIC ORGASM

Life is not about earning millions, and wealth is not an unforeseeable concept. You must find your own definition of wealth that suits your needs and values. We all have a unique journey to find and align with the gifts that sit silently hidden within ourselves. We can embark on our rightful path when we awaken our energy systems.

I call it a Cosmic Orgasm because there's no feeling like that of breaking free of your Millionaire Karma, fulfilling your cosmic mission, and being able to experience life with its endless possibilities.

—STEFANIE

CHAPTER 11

THE WELL OF SOURCE IS THE SOURCE OF WEALTH

ROBIN MULLIN

—Founder of Wisdom Circles LLC and President of
the Inside Edge Foundation for Education

Aladdin had Genie. Cinderella had Fairy Godmother. Luke Skywalker had the Force. Throughout history and in all cultures, myths and stories relate how invisible helpers make wishes come true for those with sincere hearts.

We each have invisible help and our own version of a magic wand or magical creative force to support us. It is called many things including the Universe, Divine Intelligence, the Great Mystery, or the Wild Unknown. My name for this infinite pool of possibilities is the Well of Source. It is the point of origin for wealth and well-being. When we partner with it, we have infinite potential.

Wealth, to me, is not a large bank account or an accumulation of physical items. True wealth is the ability to create whatever is needed in true alignment with my soul's best life. A wealthy life includes holistic well-being on all levels: physical, mental, emotional, and spiritual.

I've learned that connecting to Source is a choice, like dipping your cup into a well. And the well is available in direct proportion to the attention you invest in it. With sincere intention, commitment, and clumsy practice, my relationship with Source has become strong. Building a consistent relationship with my Well of Source has helped me to magnetize homes, jobs, relationships, creative ideas, and amazing experiences beyond my wildest dreams! In sharing my journey, I want to inspire other WILD women to enhance their own relationship with the Well of Source. I'll share techniques I've used to gain wealth and expanded well-being with increased speed, ease, and joy.

THE GIFT OF MYSTICAL EXPERIENCES

Being open to experiences beyond our understanding can jolt us into a new way of seeing the world. As we learn to stay present and embrace glimpses of situations beyond linear time and space, we begin to know the wisdom of the Well of Source. At several pivotal points in my life, unexpected and unexplainable events grabbed my attention and demanded I consider a new perspective.

Such mystical experiences are portals to encounters that take us beyond our current edge of knowledge. Each of the dozens of times they have occurred for me, I was in a transition point in my life where I was asking for clarity with a sincere inquiry in my heart. My first two encounters happened at the age of twenty-four. Newly unemployed, in an abusive relationship, and feeling lost, I spent my savings on a trip to Egypt and Israel. I couldn't explain it, but I knew I needed to go on this trip with a small group led by my first yoga teacher, Sharon Warren. After a week of freedom from any usual routines, I was feeling relaxed as I was sitting near the Saqqara Pyramid. As I sifted through the sand like a child on a beach, I was surprised to find a milky-quartz crystal about six inches long. I held it and closed my eyes to rest as I waited for my friends. Suddenly, I felt transported back in time to a hallway inside an ancient stone temple. I moved through walls to different rooms where I observed healing practices that used sound to tune organs of the body. When I shared this "dream" with our Egyptian guide, he told me there was a myth that Saqqara was the site of an underground healing temple long ago.

A week later, at the Church of the Beatitudes near the Sea of Galilee, I was given an emotional jolt that was more difficult to experience but helped me make a leap in consciousness. I was gazing at the simple altar in the center of the small chapel. When I closed my eyes, the face of Mother Mary appeared to me with open arms. My heart began pounding, and an overwhelming sense of sadness filled me and grew into uncontrollable crying. I sobbed for an hour with tears of compassion for all the pain and suffering in the world. I am deeply grateful for both transformational gifts that reminded me I am not alone. These encounters with the divine mystery or Source gave me courage to make difficult, life-changing decisions, including ending my abusive relationship and moving to California.

The unexplainable experiences did not scare me. They seemed familiar and comforting in a way. This is likely because my earliest years allowed a prolonged period during which the veil was thin between this world and the unseen energetic world that continually surrounds us. Because I was born with sight labeled "legally blind," I developed other senses more fully. I lived in my beautiful, blurry world for two-and-a-half years, seeing color, light, and energy, but no defined shapes. I knew people as orbs of pulsating color that got larger as they approached me. I learned the smells of places, like my grandparents' house that was a mixture of baking bread, Ivory soap, and pipe tobacco. Learning to depend on a variety of unseen perceptions, including vibrational energy and sensing emotions, helped me feel comfortable without sight.

My first pair of eyeglasses opened a new way of seeing. I am told that I would sit for hours on the grass outside, amazed to discover individual blades of grass, leaves, and tiny bugs. But I also recall being relieved each night when I could take off my glasses and return to my familiar world of light shows and dancing colors. Blurred lines and connection were familiar friends that reminded me I was part of something beautiful, beyond the definition of lines. Relying on sensing energy and intuition as a child has served me well in navigating various states of consciousness as an adult.

MAGNETIZING WONDERFUL OUTCOMES

Consciously connecting with the resources of the Well of Source energy helps magnetize outcomes in tangible forms as well as experiences. When I ask for help getting something my soul is longing to have, I usually have no idea how to make it happen. What fun it is to watch how my requests take form a step at a time. Often, they are more spectacular than I imagined. Once while visiting Hawaii, I got chills when I saw a house that had shown itself to me in a recent dream. At the time, we had no intention of buying a house in a rural, old plantation town, but my intuition told me otherwise. An unexpected financial gift from family showed up to make the purchase possible. Looking back now, I realize that buying that house set in motion eight years of soul-shifting experiences that brought many more tangible outcomes including improved health, important friendships, and a new career path for me.

Circumstances suddenly changed when we needed to return to California and find a larger home with room for my mother-in-law. In 2014, the depressed housing market would mean selling at a big loss. Meanwhile, my new home wish list put buying way beyond our budget. Again, I gave the challenge to the Well of Source and waited. Very soon I learned from a new acquaintance about a home exchange website. I wrote to six California homeowners about the possibility of a trade. Within two days, one responded whose house was a perfect size in my ideal location, and we happily traded houses for four years.

The speed and ease of attracting both physical and holistic wealth have increased as I have made building a strong relationship with the Divine Source a priority. I tend to it like a sacred marriage and have made a vow to honor and respect the unseen forces that care for me. As I pay attention, listen, express my heart, and give gratitude, wealth flows more easily to me. When I am experiencing life most abundantly, I am aligned with my soul and something infinitely larger. I share below some specific techniques that I use to help keep myself in right relationship with my Well of Source:

Keeping the Channel Clear

Maintaining a pipeline free of mental and emotional debris requires us to routinely remove obstructions that keep us from our true alignment. We each will find ways that work best for us to do this. My personal clearing practices include daily time in silence and meditation, journaling, sunset walks, creating art, and periodic extended time in nature. Others dance, play music, write poetry, or practice a sport. Anything that quiets your mind and centers you is a valid clearing tool.

A clear channel helps us give and receive easily, allowing universal love to flow through us and into the world. As we radiate harmony, joy, happiness, health, beauty, healing, and compassion, we generate movement of energy toward ourselves, others, and desired outcomes.

Keep Blessings Circulating

Though our culture often gives us fear-based messages to hold and accumulate riches, doing so can block the flow of new love and wealth coming our way. Imagine breathing in and out wealth energy. Clinging too long to old air or stagnant energy is counterproductive. We need continual fresh flow for health in body, mind, and spirit. And we also benefit from circulating our gifts, ideas, kindness, and wealth. I believe that granting blessings is as important as being open to receive them; it keeps Source energy circulating. When we are filled with gratitude and joy, there is a natural desire to share. Spreading blessings every day feels wonderful and keeps the wealth energy flowing.

Listening to Guidance

Universally, spiritual masters teach that mindfulness or conscious awareness is key to individual happiness and collective harmony. Evolving consciousness requires excellent communication. Begin with careful listening as the foundation of a good friendship, a strong marriage, and a fulfilling parenting experience. Listening with attention, keen interest, and curiosity is also critical to a blissful relationship with Source.

The world around us is always in conversation, inviting us to listen and join in. Cultivating ways to hear whispers of guidance gives access to all kinds of information and support. Because tuning into Source messages through silent retreats or vision quests has proved so important for me, I chose to teach my children about it early on. Close to their tenth birthday, I introduced the concept of listening to inner and outer guidance and took each child on a first vision quest trip.

Dreamwork has been another powerful listening tool that I trust to guide me. I began working with dreams in my early twenties and have worked in dream groups for over thirty years. I am fascinated by how our subconscious cleverly uses the language of symbols and images to offer insights into current situations and provide creative ideas and new perspectives. Sometimes dreams also give us a glimpse into the future. My dreams have signaled changes coming, provided me warnings, given me glimpses of people I would meet, and have provided answers to important questions. Recently, I was wondering if having a new business partner would be a good idea. A dream gave me a clear yes to this question. It showed me a huge double fireplace inside a beautiful lodge where people gathered. The twin fires ignited together, and the flames grew at the same rate until they filled the fireboxes. When I became concerned in the dream that the fires would get out of control,

85

they became smaller in response to my thoughts. This image provided confirmation that the partnership I was considering would fuel our creativity, have equal contribution, and not get out of control. So far this has proven true.

DO YOU FEEL THE CALL?

It is up to each of us to refine our personal relationship with the Well of Source. Our listening expands as we pay attention, keep the channel clear, circulate blessings, and develop new ways to receive messages. Trust what comes from guidance and stay faithful to your relationship with Soul and Source. Holding rigidly to any particular result limits your possibilities. Make clear requests and let go of trying to control how it will show up. It is so much fun to see how Source delivers wealth in amazing ways! To complete, express your gratitude. I love this reminder from my spiritual mentor, Carolyn Conger: "What is yours will come to you. Just say 'thank you' for everything that comes."

In response to the challenges and needs of our time, many of us are feeling called to mobilize our talents. It is up to us, my WILD women sisters, to bestow our wisdom and blessings to be in service in unique new ways. I believe that modern women will be the ones to change the world. We are the ones we have been waiting for. Finding other WILD sisters who are kindred spirits will amplify the joy, wealth, and impact of everyone committed to share the journey together.

I invite you to claim your wealth through conscious partnership with Source. Walking your own path, you will delight in discovering unique ways to enhance your physical, mental, emotional, and spiritual well-being. With intention, tools, and some practice, your life can be elevated to a higher vibrational level as you give your gifts and receive with gratitude. Living a life in sacred relationship with the Well of Source is as magical as having a genie lamp or texting a message to your Fairy Godmother!

—ROBIN

CHAPTER 12

ANCESTRAL WEALTH

GENEVIEVE SEARLE

—The Optimizatoin Queen, Speaker,
and Bestselling Author of *Embrace Your Feminessence*

There is a wealth available to all of us which is rarely spoken of but runs so deep it tracks back to the dawn of humanity—our Ancestral Wealth. This is an inheritance that goes far beyond finances and remains when we have nothing else to draw on. But, like great treasure chests, sometimes we need to unlock our ancestral stories to find the gold within.

Intergenerational trauma was first suggested to me at a time when I'd been struggling emotionally for years. I'd been at the edge of depression for a long time even though I'd tried everything—from modern and herbal medicine to psychology and rebirthing retreats. Despite supportive friends, family, a loving partner, and three amazing sons, I struggled.

Yes, I had my own sexual abuse and rape to process. Yes, I'd had PTSD, blackouts, and eating disorders to heal. I felt like I had moved through so much yet, even after so long, I was still not shining fully. Why?

One day, a beautiful friend whispered, "Are you sure this is all yours?" My body tingled with a full-body *knowing*, yet my mind rejected the possibility that it couldn't be all mine because I knew of no science-backed pathway for this.

Years later, I was simultaneously studying the epigenetic effects of environmental factors—like light and electromagnetic fields—on the body as well as doing a year-long spiritual mentorship where we "tracked" our maternal lineage. I started putting two and two together, leading me to explore intergenerational and transgenerational epigenetics. Suddenly, so much of my life experience that hadn't made sense before did so now.

Epigenetics is the science of how we interact with the world around us: how our environment, experiences, thoughts, and behaviors influence the way our genes work and process information. It works above the gene, not altering genes themselves, but altering their expression. Much like a light switch, it turns a light on or off but doesn't change the actual wiring.

Epigenetics is a dynamic, real-time process where our bodies are constantly assessing and responding to our environment and preparing for the future. Everything—including food, light, temperature, habits, relationships, and thoughts—influences it.

UNRAVELLING MY MOTHERLINE

My grandmother's life was full of broken dreams, grief, loss, and virtual exile from her community. In her final three years, she was denied access to her five children. She died of pancreatic cancer, heartbroken and alone only months after her thirty-sixth birthday. I arrived twelve years later on the exact day my grandmother would have turned forty-eight. This synchronicity is not lost on me.

I feel a soul connection with the woman whose eyes I never saw, whose birthday I share, and whose stories I carry in my bones. At another time, with more resources and different cultural awareness, my grandmother's unique radiance and desire for a full, free life might be celebrated. Instead, she lost everything for daring to dream and being bold enough to try. One day I hope to tell her story, honoring her legacy as a WILD woman born too early for the world.

My mother forged a beautiful life despite losing her mother at only sixteen and her own early trauma. She raised three children, travelled the world, and only recently retired from her successful psychology practice. My father has always been a great support to her; however, I don't feel my mother has ever truly *thrived*.

My mother and grandmother's stories of grief, loss, trauma, abuse, and abysmal self-worth then passed to me, not intentionally but epigenetically.

Before I even emerged into the world, their stories had been *epigenetically imprinted* onto my DNA.[1] As an egg inside the ovaries of my mother, while she still grew in my grandmother's womb, I vicariously experienced both of their lives; their environment, relationships, experiences, and yes, traumas, were all experienced by me.

Encoded into my system was my grandmother's story. I experienced this fear as, "If I'm too big, bold, or different, I'll lose everything, be outcast from my community, and die alone."

This fear ran through me unconsciously for many years. If I dared step out, shine, or stand my ground, my body would "contract" into self-loathing. I'd be overwhelmed with a sense of "wrongness," my anxiety skyrocketing, all leading to high-functioning depression. I'd develop vaginal thrush, intestinal parasites, and constipation without changing my diet. Scoliosis and spondylolisthesis in my spine also caused issues with my gut and feet. Scoliosis is often inherited, and I believe my spine's curvature reflects an internal push-pull between being myself and conforming to belong.

OUR BODIES TELL THE STORIES

Intergenerational trauma is becoming more widely recognized. It's relatively easy to study because big events like the Holocaust and the Dutch Famine provide clear beginnings and families can be fairly easily traced.[2] But what about when there's no direct link, such as when the father is an unknown sperm donor? Does his experience get passed down too?

Research suggests yes. If deemed important enough, imprints can cross into subsequent generations—even when there's no contact with the original person.[3] In the Cherry Blossom Mouse Study, male mice were repeatedly traumatized with electric shocks that they associated with the scent of cherry blossom. Two generations later, their offspring (via artificial insemination) not only experienced a trauma response when they smelled cherry blossom, but they were also born with extra neurons in their nose to detect the scent earlier, giving future generations a better chance at avoiding potential danger.[4]

Like the mice, our bodies tell the stories of our lives and the lives of those that came before us. We are walking anthology books stretching back to the dawn of humanity.

GOING BEYOND SURVIVAL

As I pieced together my own experience, ancestral story, scientific research, and spiritual awareness, I began to look beyond trauma. Surely, if we carry negative imprints, we must also carry positive ones.

Healing trauma is vitally important; however, the true richness lies in going beyond surviving to *thriving*. When we alchemize our own story and our ancestral stories into our biggest gifts, the whole game changes. This is the kind of *wild* wealth that no one talks about.

Like living elixirs, we are unique blends of our ancestry, experiences, and environments. As we enhance certain attributes through awareness and aligned action, we alter the molecular structure of this elixir—ourselves. With this knowledge, we can change negative patterns, limiting beliefs, and maybe even physical traits. By alchemizing them, we can tap into our inner wealth and actualize our Soul Purpose.

I needed to heal the story of my motherline; but more than that, I wanted to honor these women by living a life they never even dreamt of—soulful connections, rich experiences, joy, and prosperity is how I define a wealthy life. Sharing my wisdom, inspiring others, and helping with the evolution of humanity through speaking, writing, and mentoring is my Soul Purpose. To create this, I needed to access additional traits and characteristics that they didn't have.

UNCOVERING HIDDEN TREASURE

I believe when we see other people shining with a trait or characteristic and deeply desire it, it's because it already lies unacknowledged within us. When I looked forward to what I desired to create and considered what characteristics I needed to enhance for this, it was my Aunt Narelle who held the key.

Bold, creative, entrepreneurial, and always dazzling anyone who crossed her path, Narelle launched twenty iconic restaurants in her life. She wears bright orange hats, layers of self-designed jewellery, and recently painted the pillars in her Bali home magenta. Because she's lived a "high life," I rejected her, taking this as a lack of depth, but I was wrong. She has a lot of love and remarkable resilience, even after losing three life partners. Her tenacity inspires me.

This totally fabulous woman offers a legacy of unapologetic self-expression, business savviness, playfulness, and proof that anything is possible . . . and that this is all woven into my bones. I lean into this knowing that her strengths are imprinted into me. My job is taking this incredible blend of qualities, along with the myriad of others that have been passed down through the generations, to craft my own unique elixir.

My parents gifted me compassion, depth, ethics, and an ability to discern patterns in a way that many people miss; my maternal grandmother, through her tragic story, granted me curiosity, courage, and commitment. When I layer this with the audacity, savviness, and sparkle of my aunt, I have a potent combination indeed!

ANCESTRAL ALCHEMY

How did I work to heal the negative and enhance the positive? By reverse engineering what's known about trauma to support my own growth and evolution.

Imprints seem to happen through:

- An event so big that we are forever changed from it, and/or
- Repeated behaviors or experiences

By working with Ceremony and Ritual, I intentionally created big experiences supported by repeated behaviors to create new imprints. Ceremony is designed to grab the attention by creating an experience that's very different than normal, making both our conscious and unconscious mind focus intently on what's unfolding. I believe this is its true power and gold. Ritual is simply intentional repetition.

Combining Ceremony and Ritual together with the power of non-linear movement—like ecstatic dance—created a pathway for healing, positive repatterning, and personal evolution not only in my mind but also in my body.

Over the years, I've internally alchemized some big ancestral stories by incorporating these techniques. The imprint from my grandmother that it wasn't safe to be free and shine has been one of the biggest to overcome.

Whenever I reach a point in my own growth where I need to level-up so I can live my fullest potential and actualize my Soul Purpose, I ask myself this: *Who holds the epigenetic codes for the traits I need to enhance?* Then I consciously imprint this into my whole being—body, mind, heart, and spirit.

Too often we hand our power over to others, but the truth is, we have everything we need already encoded within us. We are far more powerful than we've been led to believe.

I invite you to ask yourself:

- How do I uniquely need to eat, move, breathe, socialize, work, and live to thrive and shine?
- What ancestral stories do I carry?
- How can I turn these into my greatest assets?

The answers to these offer you true wild wealth and are available to you because they live within you!

To access this, I combine:

- Ph360 Epigenetic and Hormonal Profiling—a cutting-edge, science-based artificial intelligence technology offering precise and personalized wellness advice in six key areas: food, movement, relationships, work, environment, and natural talents based on a person's dominant hormones
- Ancestral Alchemy—family history "tracking," Ceremony, and Ritual
- Embodied Movement and Functional Breathing—rebalances the nervous system and reprograms both body and mind
- Soul Work

LIVING ELIXIRS OF POTENTIAL

We each come from millions of people dating back to the dawn of humanity, and through this we carry built-in archetypes—archetypes you can work with to draw your latent traits to the fore. Who lives in your family tree? Who in your ancestry already has the imprints for the traits you need to embody to step into your fullest potential? You don't have to like them as a person or endorse how they live for them to carry a key for your evolution. Instead, take the essence of what they offer and do it your way.

You are the distilled essence of all who came before you, a potent elixir crafted from more than a thousand generations. Your ancestral stories are waiting to be told through you in a whole new way. Knowing who you are, where you came from, and how to access the treasure trove of gifts that already live within you is key to being able to unlock true wealth.

This is what gives you the knowledge and power to move through obstacles and limitations. This is what holds the key to your health, relationships, personal power, financial success, and Soul Purpose. Your true wild wealth is *within* you! Unlock it!

— GENEVIEVE

NOTES:

1. Irene Lacal and Rossella Ventura, "Epigenetic Inheritance: Concepts, Mechanisms and Perspectives," *Front Mol. Neurosci* 11, no. 292 (September 2018). https://doi.org/10.3389/fnmol.2018.00292

2. Natan Pf Kellermann, "Epigenetic transmission of Holocaust trauma: can nightmares be inerhited?" *Isr J Psychiatry Relat Sci* 50, no. 1 (23013). http://pubmed.ncbi.nlm.nih.gov/24029109; Bastiaan T. Heijmans, Elmar W. Tobi, Aryeh D. Stein, and L.H. Lumey, "Persistent epigenetic differences associated with prenatal exposure to famine in humans," *Proceedings of the National Academy of Sciences* 105, no. 44 (September 2008). https://doi.org/10.1073/pnas.0806560105

3. Lundi Ly, Donovan Chan, Jacquetta M Transler, "Developmental windows of susceptibility for epigenetic inheritance through the male germline," *Semin Cell Dev Biol* 43 (July 2015).

4. Brian Dias and Kerry Ressler, "Parental olfactory experience influences behavoir and neural structure in subsequent generations," *Nat Neurosci* 17, (2014) https://doi.org/10.1038.nn3594

CHAPTER 13

MANIFESTING WEALTH

ANIA HALAMA

—Host of the *Spirituality for Badass Babes* Podcast, Cofouner of Project Save the Toads, Reiki Master, EFT and *Ho'oponopono* Master, and Intuitive Healer

I grew up fairly poor with a learned attitude from my family's perspective that stemmed from the old saying, "Money doesn't grow on trees." It's acceptable to say that I grew up having deep, limiting beliefs around money and believing that I'd probably continue living poorly for the rest of my life. I remember thinking to myself, *If my parents are poor, how could I be wealthy?* I had to work on that feeling, sit with it, and unlearn it. This wasn't easy—reprogramming your mind from something that you've known your entire life can be daunting, scary even. But to be wealthy is to do something uncomfortable, to unearth wealth within on a spiritual level, truly embodying all there is and having the balance of spiritual, mental, emotional, physical, relational, and financial wealth within yourself. Once you are fully balanced, the financial wealth will come. Eventually I realized that I am worthy because worthiness is a birthright.

I started to notice my family's income deficiencies when I was very young (around second or third grade), usually in moments when we couldn't afford discounted lunches or spend a little extra on brand name foods, resorting to the cheapest possible options. We were immigrants from Poland and had come to America when I was three. My parents didn't speak a word of English, which landed them a few odd jobs, some even having them clean offices and houses just to pick up some extra work due to their language barriers. My parents did the very best they could. There came a day when a lot had to change when my dad faced an unfortunate injury from his job as a welder, leaving him handicapped in one arm and unable to work. I remember translating legal and medical documents at the age of ten because I was the only one learning English from school. I had to step up and be an adult to help my parents.

By the age of sixteen, I had a full-time job. I had taken a graphic design class in high school and unearthed a passion for it. It landed me an internship followed by a corporate job after earning my bachelor's at nineteen. By the age of twenty, I was making six figures. I was the first one of my friends that had a "big girl" job, and I was very generous with my money, always believing that it will come back to me if I spend it with good intention. This is still a belief that I have to this day: put the energy out there that you want to receive back. But being a twenty-year-old, I spent most of my money on drugs, alcohol, and fancy purses. When my dad started seeing the money I was bringing in, he began stealing from me. This took me down a dark path of hatred, substance abuse, ailments, and more. A constant agony lived in my head—*Why did he do this to me?*—and anxiety built up within me that I couldn't show the outside world. It took a long time until I was able to forgive him.

STRESS SICK

By twenty-three, I grew physically and mentally sick from the high stress of my job and everything going on at home. I was dealing with anxiety, insomnia, depression, celiac disease, and dense, dark energies. By twenty-five, I had grown so terribly ill I was going blind, and doctors couldn't figure out what was wrong with me. My body was deteriorating from the inside; this was my final straw. I realized that if I didn't have my health, I had nothing else. No money in the world could replace that.

I soon stepped away from graphic design because I was so jaded and didn't enjoy designing for corporate America. I wasn't allowed to be creative or make beautiful art—everything had to be masculine and structured when art is flowing and feminine. On top of that, if I didn't have my vision, I wouldn't be able to design years down the line. Something needed to change. I was fed up. I decided to quit everything and travel the world. I had to get as far away as I could from my hometown (Chicago).

I started in Southeast Asia, making my way to Europe, and ending in South America. Living abroad was cheaper, so I had more money to spend on meditation, yoga, and personal development classes. I started to self-heal through Eastern medicine practices and modalities like meditation and reiki (healing through universal life force energy), which inspired me to become certified in both. When I reached South America, I started experimenting with plant medicines. Plant medicines are one of the biggest catalysts to my growth today. I was able to disconnect myself from the physical world and turn inward into my spiritual world. I came to the realization that you can have all the money in the world but if your inner self isn't at peace, you will never be happy. Though it took some time, I was able to heal my insomnia, anxiety, and stress levels. I was also able to understand myself since I was never granted that time due to growing up fast and taking on adult responsibilities at an early age. I was on a path to a deeper connection with my soul.

ATTRACTING MY DESIRES

Before I began my spiritual journey, I was dating a man who was manifesting money left and right. I was amazed. So naturally, I convinced him to teach me his ways. He was well over twenty years into his spiritual journey, and I was just starting. Coming from a corporate background, my interest in earning more money was already present from the hustling masculine energy I was tapping into all the time. I didn't exactly know how to harness the feminine energy, nor was I aware of the spiritual aspect of attracting wealth from feminine energy. I didn't know that money is energy, and like most people, I thought that money was objectively something we work for. When I saw the way he was attracting money and great opportunities into his life, I started meditating, working closely with him, and learning more about the laws of the universe, including the law of attraction—the belief that anything that you think of (positive or negative) can manifest into existence. I was able to reprogram a lot of my thinking and leaned into attracting my desires rather than chasing them. I was then introduced to Emotional Freedom Technique (EFT) tapping.

EFT tapping is simple and accessible to all. It allows us to move energy in our bodies to instill a new set of beliefs. It's the focus on meridian points in our bodies, just like in acupuncture; however, instead of pinching ourselves with needles, we tap those points with our fingers. We do cycles of mantras that start with negative affirmations and end with positive affirmations. You'd start with the side of the hand, then between your eyebrows, side of the eye, under the eyes, under the nose, chin, collar bone, and so on. There's no right or wrong way to conduct EFT tapping; so long as you are hitting the points and starting with the negative affirmations and ending with positive ones, you'll be able to see a shift in your energy right away. I watched my boyfriend do EFT tapping on himself daily. At first, I thought it was cuckoo, which didn't work positively in my favor. Remember when I mentioned the law of attraction (like attracts like)? Due to that initial skepticism, I wasn't seeing any results. I kept "trying and trying," but did not feel any shift in energy.

I soon learned that our intentions and trust have a lot to do with any practice because we are required to be open to the possibilities. I was still very high anxiety at this point. My boyfriend convinced me to do one full session with him specifically around anxiety where the only stipulation was that I had to give it my full faith that it will work. Okay, what did I have to lose?

We sat in the session and started out with some breathing exercises that followed the tapping series. Before I knew it, the anxiety started to wither away, and BOOM! All of a sudden, all my anxiety went away. It felt like all my problems I'd been carrying for years just disappeared in that exact moment, and I finally turned to peace within. It's at that moment that I surrendered my trust from my internal mind to the possibilities of what could be that I saw a shift. I kept waiting for the anxiety to come back, but it never did. It's as if I was working with some kind of magic.

LIMITING BELIEFS

Today, I am certified in several practices including EFT tapping, Ho'oponopono, Akashic records, reiki, and more. I believe that we should teach from experience. Because of my experience growing up, I frequently help my clients with limiting beliefs that I once had as well. The most common limiting beliefs I see in entrepreneurs that come to me for help are worthiness issues—feeling unworthy of money, success, or more clients. I'm also a law-of-attraction coach, so

I don't teach people how to work hard to get the money; I lean toward helping them merge their masculine and feminine energies to manifest money and ideal clients. One of my favorite things is teaching people how to depend on their energies to manifest their desires, rather than constantly hustling. In a way, I help entrepreneurs by incorporating healthy spiritual practices into their lives.

I know how to hone in and do well with seeing tangible results from my law-of-attraction methods—like the time I manifested $100,000 in just forty days. You do this by focusing on exactly what you want and none of the things you don't want. Remember, your thoughts attract your reality. If you have just one slip up of a thought like, *I don't know how I'm going to do that,* or *$100,000 is a lot of money,* this will set you back on your manifestations. This is when EFT tapping comes in real handy to reprogram your mind from any of those negative thoughts that pop up. I help clients fulfill their manifestation goals, and it's been a fantastic journey to watch them grow from their limitations and attract their rightful successes.

REDIRECT YOUR PASSIONS!

With my business, Rebel Entrepreneur, growing at the rate it has so far, I have decided to focus on the spiritual and enlightened side of my coaching and working with everyday people to connect with their souls and find their purpose. The idea of hosting my own in-person retreats came to me and reenergized my passion for my work—gathering people for plant medicine ceremonies, hikes, and various relative spiritual practices.

This boost of passion also gave me the idea to host my own summits. The events feature fifteen speakers—five speakers a day—who all delved further into the many ways we can connect to our energy and harness our abilities in all things, supporting growth and transformation. I've found myself gravitating toward the healing work of helping my community align with their spiritual selves to bring their wildest ideas into their physical realities.

Today, it feels so good to be based in Medellin, Colombia. I am surrounded by my wonderful friends and fellow spiritual entrepreneurs. Together, we exchange many healing sessions while continuing with our manifestations. In fact, I've taken note of my manifestations and the funny ways that they effortlessly fall into my lap. More recently, my two friends and I decided to partner up and create an environmental project in our efforts to save the toads.

With Project Save the Toads, we want to give back to the land by conserving the amphibians and land while doing our part in helping the infrastructures of our jungles. I believe to be wealthy, we have to be in service—always. The universe works in miraculous ways and when we help those less fortunate (whether that's people or animals) the higher powers repay us in beautiful ways. As soon as we set our intentions with this project, the opportunities to expand on our idea came forth. One of my partners and I went to a conference in Miami where we met with three hundred investors who were very thrilled about our mission. It was all in such perfect alignment, inspiring us to continue to go bigger.

YOU HAVE THE POWER TO MANIFEST WEALTH

I credit most great things that have come my way to focusing on wealth from a spiritual level. It's important to look internally and unearth the wealth within, finding that all opportunities and possibilities can effortlessly come to us when we are tapping into the flowing energy and the state in which we can attract all things perfectly—and abundantly—in divine timing.

I guess I can say that it's easy to continue building on the success of my business, writing three soon-to-be-published books, launching an environmental activism project, and surrounding myself with a community of loving people when I'm nourishing my spiritual wealth.

—ANIA

PART IV

CHOICES BECOME EMPOWERMENT

CHAPTER 14

THE WEALTH OF PERSONAL FULFILLMENT

TARRYN REEVES

—CEO of Four Eagles Publishing and *USA Today* Bestselling Author

Wealth is about making money—lots of it. Make it. Accumulate it. Spend it. Flaunt it. Wealth is financial and so very shallow. Wrong.

Wealth isn't just about money—it's the decisions you make, how you choose to spend your time, and how you nurture your relationships and yourself. It's the freedom to choose where you exert your freedom of choice. We grow up and make our way through life believing that wealth is about money. Of course there is that side to it, but it is so much more than that.

Wealth is made up of so many parts: our finances, our health, our mindset, our emotions, our experiences, our relationships—all areas of our life. We can create wealth in these areas, or we can leave ourselves destitute. The choice really is ours, and our lives are our greatest works of art. So instead of choosing to sign up to such a shallow view of money and all the negativity that goes along with it (money-is-the-root-of-all-evil squad, I'm looking at you!), I choose to look at wealth in a more joyful and encompassing light full of possibilities.

My motto is, "Inspire. Impact. Ignite." What we teach is what can be created. The truth is that I feel the most wealthy when I make a list of all the things I have that money can't buy. My experiences and memories are priceless. To be able to choose and prioritize more of these moments is to have wealth beyond measure. This is my truth. As humans, we are consuming machines. We're always trying to upgrade our homes, phones, and faces—it's madness. Do you ever stop to think about why you may be acquiring so much? Are you upgrading all these things because they enrich you, or because you want to feel better about yourself? I know that I was a regular prisoner of this consumer system. Whenever I felt uncomfortable (God, not those pesky feelings again!), it was off to the shops I went. Books are my personal favorite thing to buy when I need that quick dopamine hit! I have come a long way since my mindless, zombie-like shopping days, but I still sometimes look up and think, *Oops! Here I am again!* We all do it, and there is nothing wrong with buying what you desire. What I want to encourage is for us to become more aware of our actions and to live our lives filled with deeper understandings of ourselves. I wish for you, dear reader, to have not only financial wealth, but to be wealthy in every single area of your life. I want you to feel so wealthy and full of joy that you might just burst at the seams with happiness at any moment.

SELFLESS STEPS

The way that I see it, wealth is an infinite cycle, and paying it forward—in my opinion—is our responsibility. When I felt stressed or anxious, I'd turn to acquiring things, and it was instant dopamine. There was a sigh of relief with each purchase, but the pain within myself, whatever feeling I was trying to escape from, never stayed away for long. Living this way was not sustainable. I realized the quick fixes of endorphin releases were prolonged in a healthy manner when I took more selfless steps like spending quality time with my daughter, sending a message to a friend to make them smile, or getting outside and growing something! Instead of looking outside of myself for fulfillment, I began to look within. Lo and behold, it really is true what all the gurus say: everything I need is already inside of me if I am willing to be uncomfortable and courageous enough to look.

FULLY YOU

The magic begins when you realize that the cage you find yourself in was built by you. The door is open, and you can just, well, simply walk out! Leave that cage behind. Yes, it may feel like comfort, but it isn't. It's a trap. One designed to keep your brilliance hidden.

My love, you are a work of art. You were not made to be hidden. You were made to show up and have the audacity to be all of you! The shiny, the messy, the chaotic, the beautiful, the mesmerizing being that makes you special. Many of us grow up and exist in an environment that tells us to not be too loud, to not be too wild, to not be too damn much! Why? Because it makes other people uncomfortable. What we need to understand here is that those feelings you may have triggered in someone else have nothing to do with your worth and everything to do with the journey or the lesson that that person must take as a result of having come in to contact with your brilliance. This is a lot to take in, I know. When I first dared to secretly peek through the open door of my cage and dip my toe into the remembrance of who I truly am and how I want to live my life, it was like tumbling into a pool of all the icky feelings. I wallowed around in my own fear, self-doubt, shame, guilt, repulsion, and grief like it was my safety net. This was the zone I had grown to feel was acceptable to live in. Yet part of me knew better, and now that I had discovered that first taste of freedom from my own hell, there was no way I was ever going back. It may sound like I am making light of this journey and that it was simple. It wasn't. It was one step forward and four hundred back. But each time I was courageous enough to let a little more of me be fully expressed, that cage got smaller and smaller. So small, in fact, that it can no longer contain me.

Sometimes I look over my shoulder with a wistful glance at that cage and have a brief moment of insanity, wishing I was back in the comfort of its embrace because, let's face it, fully expressing yourself in a society that tells you not to is hard. But you and I are designed to do hard things, my love.

WOMEN CREATING WEALTH

Part of my brand is connected to my passion for women starting businesses and telling their stories, which make an impact. When women make good money, they don't typically run to buy the latest luxury cars, yachts, or holiday homes. In my experience, women are more conscious forces and invest it back into the community. That is not to say that our men are not doing good in the world too—they are. I just have more experience speaking to my female counterparts on this topic.

I like to see women finding their voices because women tend to tone their voices down to be more palatable. I like to heal that by offering women the outlet to share their stories, write books, or tell stories through their businesses and marketing strategies. Women still need to be wives, mothers, friends, sisters, and themselves at the end of each day, and I want that to be of more discussion. My passion for celebrating women is the tie-in with both my personal brand and my publishing company. By opening up the conversation, being vulnerable, going first, and telling it like it is, I hope you realize that you are not alone. That everyone has a story and that we can create a wealthy life from the inside out. It starts with the willingness to try and take it step-by-step after that.

THE COST OF SIX FIGURES

Before I became a multi-business owner, a wife, and a mother, I was climbing the corporate ladder at twenty-three, making six figures, and thinking I had it made. Society tells you that's what success looks like, but they fail to mention the other side. The other side is where I was exhibiting massive burnout, struggling with anxiety, and dealing with past traumas, all while keeping it together for a job. My self-worth was reflected by what I could achieve, and if I wasn't achieving something, then I wasn't good enough. It was as if I couldn't just exist. I continue doing the work today of unlearning and reminding myself that it is okay to just be. Remember it is a journey back to self and not something that is going to miraculously happen overnight. The journey begins with the awareness that you want something else followed by the deep exploration of what it is that you truly desire. Not what someone tells you that you should want. Not what society tells you that your life should look like. What does your unique soul want? And so the journey begins. How exciting!

BEING A SOLOPRENEUR

When I first started out as an entrepreneur, I was in a one-person band, which had me booking myself up and burning out quickly. I couldn't simply focus on being the visionary of my business. I didn't know how to ask for help, let alone receive it! Today, I find relief from that conditioning because I loosened my chokehold of control little by little and hired the right people to come into my team, and I continue to be that visionary. The power of a team shouldn't be overlooked. Everything is a choice, and it comes at a cost, whether that is your time, energy, money, or relationships.

It's important to identify your boundaries and where you thrive best in your work. You get to decide when you will take meetings in your calendar. You get to decide that you value scheduling in time to physically exercise your body. You get to decide! Isn't that amazing?!

VICTORY THROUGH VULNERABILITY

I thrive most at my job when I am practicing authenticity. I find that people are always looking for permission to be themselves, and when people see others modeling themselves unapologetically, they feel much safer doing so. It takes courage to be the one within your known circle of influence to go first, but when you do, others feel like you are giving them permission to do the same. And so they begin their journey and show the way for someone else to begin theirs. What a beautiful gift to bestow on another. We are like lights in the darkness, flickering on and shining brighter every day so that more and more lights start to ignite, and maybe one day, the world will be filled with more light than darkness.

The world needs more people to realize that they are capable. There comes a time when we realize that we cannot lounge in the victim pool forever. You make your way out, and that's a choice. It's about taking the necessary time to do the necessary work.

SELF-THERAPY AND STORYTELLING

When my clients come into a writing program with me, it's a transformational writing experience. The stories I teach people to tell are vulnerable and real, ones that they've probably never told anybody before. When I nurture and give them the platform to tell their stories, they see themselves in a different light. I know this because my clients tell me, but I've also personally undergone the powerful journey of telling my own story in *Wild Women Rising*, *Corporate Dropouts*, and *Younger Self Letters*.

I wrote about my anxiety in the latter book, and how I used to think that my anxiety made me weak or broken. I went back on my anti-anxiety medication because, without it, I wouldn't be able to continue the work in the capacity that I do today. I made the choice to choose more for myself. This is what it looks like to understand yourself deeply, to make hard choices, and to stay aligned to the path you wish to carve out for yourself.

There's so much fear in exposing your true self and your innermost thoughts and feelings, but when you do it, you discover that you didn't die, nor did your business cave, nor does your family hate you. The healing is in meeting that fear face-on; that is when it actually loses its power. Once you communicate your truth and put it out into the world, it's not just your truth anymore, and it becomes shared wisdom.

Wealth looks like committing to your physical well-being, setting boundaries, doing the deep work of understanding yourself, and showing up as all of you even when others are shying away from your light and telling you to tone it down. It is also making money and realizing that whatever you are being financially compensated for doing is service. It is your way of showing up and serving to the best of your ability. A wealthy life is one where you have the freedom of choice and the joy of fulfillment in every area of your existence. There will always be areas that need work. That is okay. Do the work, my love. That is where you find the next piece of the puzzle.

— TARRYN

CHAPTER 15

NURTURING SUCCESS

EBONY SWANK

—Founder and CEO of Swank A Posh

A simple truth I try to instill in my daughters—and by extension my company—is for women to be unapologetically themselves, to embrace who they are. Life's too short to be ashamed of the choices we make and the circumstances that led to them. I don't take losses lying down; every setback and every failure is an opportunity for me to strategically plan my next move.

My failures are what nurtured my success, and I want my business, Swank A Posh, to embody that. For me, wealth is more than financial—it's the quality of our character and the passion we pour into our work. What we do with that passion, who we really are, and who we want to be has a way of revealing itself. Being a black woman in America and all the culture, history, and pain that comes with it, I knew I had a high mountain to climb. It was important for me to give these voiceless, often ignored women a platform to showcase their beauty, especially when we are so often mocked and ridiculed for just being who we are—authentic. That's what it means to be unapologetic: to stand securely in your own identity in a room full of people looking at you like you're the problem.

In the realm of fast fashion, trends are inspired by what's happening on the runway. You have a brief period of time before a trend fades and is replaced by a new one. I didn't want Swank to be labeled as something so superficial; I wanted my creative mind and business to thrive. Our pieces are inspired by designers and artists all over the fashion world.

I'm happy to design products with vendors and portions of Swank's catalog. Everything I sell is everything I've touched.

TRENDS, VERSATILITY

Versatility is what I strive for when creating pieces. It's not uncommon for women to wear shorts or tank tops in colder weather. This is why I'll create a piece that can be worn all year long. I don't shy away from trends though. In fact, they're helpful. On Instagram, waist wraps were growing in popularity, so I saw a market for them and launched my own wraps. I put my personal touch on them, so it's not only unique to Swank A Posh, but specific to my audience. For any entrepreneur, you must know where a particular market or demographic is leaning, especially in fashion. Knowing what trends are becoming everyday staples can give you the leverage to maximize profit and satisfy customers.

Therefore, learning from failures is so important if you are to collect wealth. Before monetary wealth comes, it starts with wealth of knowledge . . . from learning from your mistakes.

During the tail end of the 2009 recession, I came up with the idea for Swank A Posh and opened my first store of that year. At the time, I didn't think it would turn into a full-time career. I was trying to make ends meet for my daughter and me. In those early years, I learned quickly that life doesn't stop for anyone. The clothes I was selling weren't turning a profit. The money I made was paying the rent, not running a business. Around this time, I found out I was pregnant with my second daughter. Eventually, I couldn't afford to keep my store open. I closed Swank's doors, and shortly after, my mother had a heart attack.

RESILIENT MOTHERS

To be a black mother is to be resilient. The sacrifices we make for our children are great. We sweat, bleed, and give up so much of ourselves so they can have the comfort we didn't. We cultivate their future and happiness and pray our efforts are enough to compensate for our mistakes. My mother was no different. Her love and unconditional support were a constant that I relied upon. She helped me raise my daughters.

When my mom had her heart attack, I didn't think she would make it. The doctors explained the blood flow was obstructed, and she would need triple bypass surgery if she were to have any hope of recovery. The realization my mom was dying wasn't anything I could prepare for. I felt robbed; she was being snatched from me, and I didn't have the time I needed with her. During the hardest fights in my life, she was my rock. Here I was, going through something so painful, and my security was disrupted.

When faced with death, you realize so many things in life don't matter. Chasing luxury and having a "grind" mindset just for the sake of having it is misplaced vanity if it's not rooted in something bigger than yourself. For me, wealth comes from simple things. True wealth comes from blessings from God, who maneuvered situations for me, whose hand I felt in my life more times than I can count. Wealth was my mother's support, her love. Most importantly, though, wealth is God's mercy and kindness on me. I asked God to sacrifice my unborn child just so I could have more time with her. Ultimately, my mom's bypass surgery was successful, and a few months later, I gave birth to my daughter; I was allowed to keep both. I flew my mom from Missouri to live with me full time. But after my daughter was born, I would be back in the hospital only a week later. My daughter had intestinal malrotation, a condition that causes the intestines to twist during the early stages of pregnancy. She would need surgery. I needed rest, but my daughter was my priority. I wouldn't let her go through this alone.

My business was on my mind too. I had three people depending on me. Looking back, I think during this time my character was tested more than it ever was before. This business had to work. Who I was, my inner wealth, was put to the test. I had my two daughters and mother who needed me. The failure of my business meant letting my family down. I didn't like what that meant for me. I had my family, and I had this unwavering passion to make Swank A Posh work even though I only had $12,000 to my name. I knew the money would run out quickly if I didn't plan my next move carefully. The sleepless nights, the back-and-forth with doctors, and the uncertainty of everything made my blood boil. I wanted my daughter home. I was frustrated, but I needed to know what I would do with this business.

RENEWED, REOPENED

When the doctors said I was in the clear, I took my baby home and began scouting locations to reopen Swank A Posh. With my mom's support, I went to work.

I had some leftover inventory from before, but I needed fresh material to work with. I boarded a plane to Los Angeles with my oldest daughter and sought out vendors. With hopes and prayers, I exceeded my own expectations. I had a profitable business that saw no end to its growth. My family was taken care of too.

In 2018, my mom died. I was willing to sacrifice so much for her. What God gave me, and what I needed, was time—time with my mother, time for my daughters to get to know and love their grandmother, time for me to build a secure life for my children. My mom played a vital role in my initial success. Without her help, I wouldn't be here. Her support and love was unrelenting. Her belief in me propelled me to where I am now. I don't say that lightly. Helping me with my daughters allowed me to pour myself fully into Swank.

Today, Swank A Posh has two storefronts in Metro Detroit. I took $12,000 and turned it into a forty-million-dollar company. Swank's first store—located in a mall next to a Nordstrom—taught me what I needed to be successful. The biggest takeaway is that learning never stops. Though that first store still makes me sick, I'm not mad about it. I don't know how something so integral to my company remains such a stench I can't shake whenever I visit that mall, even after all this time. Yet it was key to many of my blessings.

Being featured in *Forbes* magazine put my company in the center of the public eye. Wealth is surrounding yourself with great people. If I can give anyone a piece of advice, it would be to surround yourself with the people who love you most. My family is my biggest motivator for everything I do. My husband, Tony, and daughters, Alaya and Bailei, give me their unconditional love and support. Mike, my broker, runs my warehouse in Los Angeles and negotiates deals with vendors. No one knows who I am there. Neither do they know I run a multimillion-dollar company. When making large orders, I'm sometimes rejected by store owners. In these times, it's Mike who ensures the vendors are as productive as possible when some don't take me, a black woman, seriously. I value having members like Mike on my team. These people are dedicated and will always stand by me, regardless of my success.

EVERYDAY WOMEN

I take pride in having Swank's models resemble everyday women. I am an observer. I know the media pushes for one kind of woman, leaving millions of beautiful women underrepresented. I made sure I was different from the flyers to the branding. If you're learning from your product and what you're putting out in the world, you'll find success. If the effort is there, the results will be too. For me, that was going on Facebook and friending people in my area. I knew they would follow back or, at the very least, see my page if I tagged them. I posted women trying on jeans on Instagram, which became my own form of clickbait in a way. That encouraged more sales from these visual try-ons.

As a businesswoman, it's important to pay attention to what's going on in the realm of the customer, and sometimes that's rejecting offers. I was approached by investors who offered me a million-dollar deal for 50 percent of my company back in 2019. I had sacrificed so much of my heart and energy into Swank, I refused to toss half of it away to out-of-touch investors who didn't know how to navigate my consumer—my community.

Looking back, I can say I never let pain paralyze me. I can't. 50-Cent summed it up best, "Every negative is a positive. The bad things happen to me, I somehow make them good. That means you can't do anything to hurt me." I live by that. Failure will always be temporary if that's at the forefront of everything I do. My work and my ambition, which keep my passion alive, will be what stands. From such a young age, my mother instilled in me a hunger to pursue what I loved, to not give up on myself. If I did, who would fight for me? Her stabilization in those early years of my business is what I wish to be for my own daughters. After all these years, looking back, I realized I've had wealth that was in my mother's love and God's love, and I'll always carry that with me.

— *EBONY*

CHAPTER 16

FREEDOM TO CHOOSE

SHAR MOORE

—Talk Show Host of *The Girlfriend Hour TV* and
Founder of the Feminessence® Movement

When we think of wealth, most people think about the monetary side. While that is a fact, I believe that freedom of choice is the most important thing to look at when defining wealth. Money allows us the freedom to choose our jobs, relationships, whether we have kids, and the foods we consume—all of which gives a sense of the wealth in our lives.

I was born in Thailand, then I moved to Australia at the age of four, and by the time I was eleven, my family—organized in a hierarchy and rooted in traditional Indian culture—engaged me to a man who was nine years older than me. My Australian stepdad, who had raised me well, found out about this tradition when I was fifteen and asked if getting married at sixteen was what I wanted to do. Nobody made me feel as though I had a choice because I was simply told that this was part of the culture. Growing up in Thailand, I had seen young girls get married all the time and thought it was normal. It was then when my stepdad asked me that I realized it wasn't all that normal after all. He reminded me that as an Australian citizen I had the option to say no, and I did. I didn't know it at the time, but it was a very important decision when I fully realized that I wanted to go to school, get a job, and meet someone naturally later. It was a pivotal moment in my life that I carry with me today because it shaped my belief that when one person believes in you, anything is possible. Here I was, six months from getting married and moving to a different country, away from everything I knew, and by a stroke of some miracle, I was presented with a path that I could claim as my own.

I had the freedom to choose. I had wealth.

I had been engaged for four-and-a-half years, had never been in the spotlight because I had to live a quiet life, and was not allowed to share my dreams or passions. This was the hierarchy of my family, not my mother, who organized all of this. Indian girls are only supposed to speak when spoken to, but when only my stepdad asked about the engagement, I said I didn't want it. Using my freedom, or my wealth, brought embarrassment to the family. So, at the age of seventeen, I moved out because I could finally choose what I wanted to be.

I've never felt more wealthy than when I turned the key to my first rental home, knowing that as I unlocked that door as a single seventeen-year-old woman, literally the entire universe was waiting for me. I began my journey and started working right away. I met my husband at my first job and had our first son when I was twenty-two. Today we have two boys who are twenty-eight and twenty-four, and our daughter is eighteen. We traveled the world and lived overseas in Thailand and Dubai, where I took many corporate jobs in the spa and hotel industry.

WEALTH OF AMBITION

These big decisions around wealth came to me when I had no formal experience, had hardly finished high school, and didn't get a college degree, but had an overflowing amount of ambition. I recall some of the wealthiest moments in my life were those like when I was sitting at an interview held in a beautiful new five-star hotel in Bangkok, and the general manager told me how much potential he saw in me despite my background and where I come from. It was one of those pivotal moments where I felt seen, and all it took was a believer to unfold the possibility of anything. His belief in me made me believe I was more than the destiny that had been dictated to me my whole childhood—that I could be more than just a wife and mum at sixteen. This spurred me to think that I could work, that I could have my own business someday.

I became the hotel's executive assistant, a job that moved me forward to future opportunities in corporate positions with other companies in Thailand and led me to eventually open my day spa in the Middle East.

When we decided to move back to Australia, I opened a fashion boutique and worked as a personal stylist. It was an amazing career and I helped women transform themselves with their upgraded style while encouraging them to feel good in new colors and clothing that suited their personalities. Unfortunately, it was a rather short-lived career, as we were indirectly affected by the Queensland floods in 2011. One minute I'm running a thriving business, and the next I'm facing bankruptcy. The whole event brought back a lot of old limiting beliefs I had about myself growing up. They stemmed from the times that I would always hear that I was "just an Indian girl," and that I should remain quiet until I fulfilled my role as a man's wife one day. The voices were loud and turned into an internal crescendo saying, "They were right, you shouldn't have started a business."

SHIFTED PATHS

As mentioned, there are many key moments in my journey that have made me feel the wealthiest in my life. My experience has been full of ups and downs, and I knew the possibility of another up wasn't far from reach. I wanted to find a way to express women's empowerment through a magazine that wasn't centered around celebrities or gossip, but directed toward real, everyday women regarding business, life stories, experiences that women have undergone, and how they shifted their paths. When I scanned the local newsstands, I couldn't find a magazine close to the concept—so I started one myself.

I've always been interested in women's empowerment. Due to the circumstances that I have been through, it is in my nature to help other women be their best versions. Nurturing women is truly ingrained in everything that I do. The freedom to choose, to embrace this idea and pursue this path, and the freedom to shine a light on other amazing women doing amazing things so they can stop being best-kept secrets, made me feel positively wealthy.

EMPOWERED PUBLISHING

I had the freedom to choose my next steps—to choose to pivot from a retail business that was facing bankruptcy to start a magazine. In that moment, I felt strong and powerful and wealthy, as I had the freedom to make that decision and not just sink with my retail business. Though I didn't have any experience in the publishing industry, I felt very empowered by the decision to create YMAG.com.au. The concept of the magazine was around women's "whys," and we began profiling women in business based on why they got out of bed every day. We ran the digital magazine for close to five years until our readers crowdfunded us to get their hands on physical copies as well. It was an amazing and collaborative moment to be taken from digital to print, and we ran the magazine for a total of nine years. We eventually moved on to publishing our current magazine, called *Feminessence*, which is geared toward women who want to tap into their feminine essence and powerful innate abilities. We publish magazines and anthology books and host retreats through my publishing company, Sharanis Publishing House, in Gold Coast, Australia.

BROUGHT HOME

One of my favorite key moments through this journey of life and creating my business is when I had the incredible opportunity to share my story on a TEDx stage. I always thought that the TEDx stage was exclusively for the people that had made it, and when I was invited to share my story, it inarguably brought everything home.

As I walked out onto the TEDx stage and stood on the famous red dot, I stood ten feet tall and felt like the wealthiest person alive. Because in that moment, I felt like I had arrived. I was finally able to share my truth and my story to many.

I can honestly say that I accidentally fell into the publishing industry, which turned into my biggest business achievement. I was going bankrupt, but I had just enough money to buy a magazine off a shelf, with a vision to change the entire landscape for women. I had neither the funds nor the knowledge and know-how.

I just knew it was something that was happening from a fiercely honest place. It wasn't just a frivolous business decision, because I felt it from a deep place within my core. I was told by my peers that I was crazy to even attempt launching print magazines since a lot of bigger magazine names were going fully digital. I barely even had the means to launch a digital magazine, but when we did, the success progressed into crowdfunding over $20,000 to print and expand. We went the opposite direction and against the grain of conventional magazine launching, which became part of our success. Another part was muting the repetitive lull of celebrities, diets, fashion, and messages that could negatively affect women, and instead replacing it all with real people and knowledge that could elevate the lives of our readers. I've been in business for seventeen years now, and I continue to generate ideas that propel our message to the world.

BANTER BEAUTIFULLY

By creating our media and profiling company, we have inadvertently created a platform to share the power of women's stories to the masses. This enables them to have the freedom to choose their deepest desires, knowing that they are backed by so many others striving for the same thing.

I'm very excited for women to look out for our upcoming live TV talk show, with a live audience of a couple of hundred people, called *The Girlfriend Hour TV,* airing midyear. The show will have a nice flow of banter between our guests who will share their stories, and will hold a space for women to proudly share their wins and challenges. It's that beautiful flow and energy that women have when they get together and know that they are in a safe space to share anything. Women have been silenced and suppressed for so long, and the show is about women controlling the narrative. I truly believe we can lift the positivity and vibration of humanity when we join together in this way.

OXYGEN OF BELIEVERS

We all have an inner GPS, also known as our intuition, that is always communicating with us. The way to know if we are going in the correct direction in life is through focusing our hearing on our GPS systems. By spending time with our thoughts, we can discover truths. Though we may dismiss them at first, they will eventually need to be explored, because that is how we are unearthing our truest wealth. I also believe in the power of community, because when you share the oxygen of people who believe in you, the more you can breathe the same yourself.

—SHAR

CHAPTER 17

SHARING TO EMPOWER

BLAIR KAPLAN VENABLES

—President of Blair Kaplan Communications, Creator of Social Media Empowerment Pillars, and Cohost of *Dissecting Success* Podcast

I thought I'd be a wine-drinking soccer mom of two by now, but in my early thirties, I became sober, had no kids, and developed a love for bird-watching. I can thank the global pandemic for that last one. I'm serious—I just started identifying birds one day with binoculars, hikes and all. I've come to accept that this isn't the life that I imagined living, but here I am living it because it's the only one I have.

I came into the world blaring and have the gift of gab, so this field was where I could utilize my God-given skills. With my background in public relations came the knowledge of how to hold space for people, to really listen, and to create a safe space for people to speak their truths and feelings. This is true wealth: having the space to be who you truly are, feel what you truly feel, and share what you want to share—the good, the bad, and everything in between. True wealth, for me, is mental wealth and being empowered to share and help others share their stories.

I have an empathetic capacity to allow people to feel heard because growing up, I wasn't very heard. I was a child of divorce. Nobody told me my dad was living with addiction, so I just assumed my dad didn't love me anymore. Imagine being a daddy's girl and your dad stops coming around. If someone would have told me, "Hey, he's sick, but he loves you anyway. He just can't show up because he's not well," perhaps that would have been a different narrative in my head. This caused a lot of anger, pain, and abandonment issues.

In my twenties, after attending a personal development workshop, I found the tools within me that allowed me to accept my father for who he was and love him, no matter what. While on a break from the workshop, I called him from a phone in a grocery store, bawling my eyes out. I shared that I love him and will accept whatever relationship he could provide me. We were both crying. We both knew that this was only the beginning of the fresh start that we both needed.

Over the years he would come from Manitoba to British Columbia to visit me. We would talk on the phone, video chat, talk online, and text. We would laugh. We would bicker. He would give me advice. He even walked me down the aisle at my wedding, alongside my mom, in August of 2017; I never thought he would have been in my life to be there for such an important milestone. At the end of 2018, we learned that my father, who was now a solid pillar in my life because of a second chance, was terminally ill. He was given up to two years to live. I was devastated and began to spiral out of control.

One thing that made me feel better was alcohol. I knew I wasn't an alcoholic, but I made terrible decisions when I drank, and I didn't like who I became. Alcohol would also make my anxiety and depression worse, which didn't help the fact that I was a walking zombie who was about to have a dead father.

Because of my father's addiction to cocaine and various other drugs, I was scared that I would go down that path since our personalities are very similar. So I made a choice—my last drink was on December 31, 2018. I began my life of sobriety the next day, January 1, 2019. And on that day, I awoke to a letter from my dad, apologizing for what had happened during my formative years and explaining his addiction to me.

MY FATHER'S REGRETS

I'm open and honest about my life. I think people should normalize being more open and sharing what they are navigating in life, which is essentially why I'm here. I'm here to help spread the wealth of sharing your story. I am here to empower you. If I can help people open those floodgates and move them through their challenges, then I feel that I'm doing my life's work. One of the ways I accomplish this is through the Global Resilience Project, a community of people who read and share stories of resilience to help them heal and navigate life's most challenging times. Upon learning about my father's terminal diagnosis, I began sharing our story with my friends over coffee, online, and at events where I learned that our story empowered the people who would hear it.

The feedback we got was positive; we were really helping people and motivating them to want to heal, seek therapy, or fix relationships in their lives. My dad and I were truly inspired and started building on the Global Resilience Project. As we got momentum, I brought my sister on to help me. We integrated this idea into a book, featuring many other people's stories about resilience. I learned that everyone has a story and that when we share what we are going through and seek advice or help, we can all get through life's challenges much easier.

Seeing that there were so many stories to be told, I went beyond the book and started the *Radical Resilience* podcast to give people an additional space to share their journeys. I believe that every story deserves to be told, so every story that gets sent to us will be shared online and possibly in future books. This community was built with a vision to collect stories of resilience and publish them in a book. The stories are bookended with my father's story of addiction and my story of forgiving him. This project was created out of a need. My dad and I wanted this book and our online movement to be a legacy piece for my dad, once he was gone.

GRIEF MEETS RESILIENCE

There are a lot of extremes to my story. The past couple of years have been some of the most turbulent times. In 2019, my grandfather passed away, I was in a car accident where I suffered from a concussion, and my husband had a heart attack a few months later and had to undergo quadruple bypass surgery. After suffering from infertility for some time, I became pregnant, but that joy was short-lived when I had a miscarriage in November 2020. About three weeks after, my father-in-law passed away after a three-week battle with cancer. And by February 2021, my mother had passed away after a three-week battle with cancer. In about a three-month window, I lost my baby, father-in-law, and mom, along with everything that I thought I knew about life. I felt like I had emotional whiplash.

My life was changing rapidly. I was in a constant state of grieving. While I was learning about people's stories of resilience through the

Global Resilience Project, I was enduring some of the hardest challenges, losses, and traumatic events. Compound grief was so prominent that it started to feel like that was just who I had become—a really sad and depressed woman who could not get off the couch. This made it very hard to work on the project, but knowing the advice shared from contributors helped me get through each day.

Almost a year after my mom passed away, I started to feel other feelings than sadness—happiness, creativity, relaxed. I started to feel like a new version of me and was ready to keep growing the Global Resilience Project.

I had started the project because my dad was terminally ill and I wanted to produce something with him in our lifetime together, but while doing so, I lost the most important members of my family. Within 360 days after my mother's death, my dad succumbed to his illness and passed away. I never thought that by the time I'd be wrapping up the first book for the Global Resilience Project, I'd also be grieving my mother, father, and the drastic changes in my life. The project has become a way for me to turn my pain into purpose. It is a way for me to feel wealthy by empowering others to share their story. Sharing our stories is a way for us all to practice mental wealth, love, and empowering each other to continue onward.

BOUNCE FORWARD

Over the years, I've learned there are certain things to do to strengthen your resilience muscles so when you need them, you can move forward. I used to define resilience as the ability to bounce back, but it is quite the opposite—it's the ability to bounce forward. If you think about it, what are you really bouncing back to? With every challenge or experience, we learn something. We don't go back to where we were because we're constantly moving forward to where we are going next.

I practice gratitude every day. I've created it into a daily ritual where I list three things I'm grateful for, at the same time, every day. Doing this for twenty-one days builds a habit to see the world more positively. I started doing this in 2016. I would set my phone alarm at 9:00 p.m., and every day my husband and I (and whomever I'm around) would list our three things from that day. I call it the Gratitude Alarm. It's a ritual that has helped me through my worst times because I'm, in a sense, forced to think about the three things that are great at the end of each day.

MINDSET PIONEER

I'm a social media marketing mentor, meaning that when I work with clients, I work with their mindsets. I started working in social media marketing before it was a profession. I've been called a pioneer or an avant-garde maven, but quite simply I'm a storyteller, and I use social media to get my clients' stories out there. There is a certain way to go into sharing your story, and I've got it down to a perfect science. It's a model that I've been modifying since 2007. It's helped me in the way that I present, market, and share my world. It's called the Social Media Empowerment Pillar, a.k.a. EMPOWER.

EMPOWER

- **Edutain:** Build content that is both educating and entertaining.

- **Money:** What is your advertising budget? How much do you want to make? Get specific with your money goals.

- **Personas:** Make content to attract your ideal customer. Whom do you wish there was more of? Create a persona for those people.

- **Other Players:** I believe in collaboration over competition. Who are your potential partners? Where are they getting PR? Maybe there's an opportunity for you to be somewhere they're not.

- **Wins:** People don't show their wins enough. If you don't share what you're capable of, how will others know what you're capable of? How will your community support you if they can't brag about you? I call it peacocking and bragging to the public. Here is where you can build your publicity strategy and get media coverage by pitching your wins to journalists and beyond. Have your expertise featured in publications, so when people find you, they know that you are credible.

- **Engagement:** Show people you're a real person behind your social media. You can't just post and ghost. Keep commenting, following, and liking. It's important to interact with your crowd.

- **Realistic Goals:** I'm all about setting goals: personal, professional, and health. If you don't know where you're going, how are you going to get there? How much money do you want to make? How much content do you want to put out? What type of content are you going to put out? How much money do you want to invest in putting out that content? Where do you want to go next?

These seven pillars are the essence of cultivating clout and becoming a thought leader. They are the pillars you need to build out so that you can authentically share who you are, what drives you, and how you will show up on social media. These empowerment pillars are the pillars that will empower you to share so that you share and empower others.

I think the most important thing to remember during building your social media presence is to show up authentically with your story. Don't worry about posting a certain number of times a day. In fact, I say, "Eff the algo!" Show up as you are. It's not always about getting five thousand likes. Surely you can Google how to make a post, but do you know how to tell your story and empower others? Ask yourself, "Do I know what my story is?"

Millions Empowered

My goal remains to be a strong and encouraging force. I want to always be empowering millions of people on a consistent basis. Funny enough, I told myself on my thirty-sixth birthday that by the time I'm forty, I want to empower eight million people. I was then booked on a TV show where the viewership was fifteen million. I then thought, "Well, I guess I should set a higher goal!" So I've humbly bumped that goal up to eighty-eight million people.

I'm just a vintage millennial . . . and I'm only at the beginning of my journey.

—*BLAIR*

PART V

THE PERSONAL BRAND OF YOU

CHAPTER 18

BECOME AN ASSET

DANELLE DELGADO

—CEO of Life Intended LLC and The Internal Alliance and
Bestselling Author of *I Choose Joy*

Everyone wants assets, but assets can be lost. If you want to build wealth, if you want to guarantee your wealth, if you want to ensure that what you build will never be taken away from you, *you* must become an asset. Who *you* are is the secret weapon.

I know you have seen it in action, probably even met them before. Those people of influence, wealth, or recognizable stature all have that *something extra*. Not simply charisma—it's beyond character. They have built a life so competently, so congruently to who they truly are that success is their way of life. They need not ever impress another, because their impact does.

What if you were the one that added value to every room you entered—the one with the most connections, a skillset few had, possessed resources many couldn't get, the best public speaker, negotiator, friend? You have the gifts right now that could build it. Your natural inclinations and talents, when magnified and trained, can lead you to be the person that is always called upon when conversations of opportunity are going down.

I want this moment of your life to be worth the time you are investing into it, and becoming the one your results require will change your life forever. It will allow you to build anything you want and live amongst the rare group designated as wealthy.

FIRST: BUILD YOURSELF

I once had a mentor tell me, "Danelle, who you are at your worst is who you are." I was shocked at first, but then it clicked.

I said, "Oh my goodness, this will make a human magical."

What if I could be my best at even my worst? What if, while enduring cancer, divorce, the losses of life, I could still win like it was my best day ever? So that is exactly the model I built and lived, and it became my rhythm. Humans who daily do the right things, practice gratitude and growth, and work on their goals become a powerhouse under pressure.

Make no mistake, it is a commitment to check daily what you need to keep doing that is working, stop doing what's not, and start doing what you know will get you where you want to be. What you build will be responsible for building you. What you don't will be what breaks you. So it's time to stop stopping. It's time to be more afraid of being nothing than of being something.

The following is my guidebook to help you build yourself into an asset. This work was the most important on my journey, and I have taught it for over a decade to thousands of others around the world. I like to call this Unstealable Everything—joy, success, money, confidence, competence, freedom, fun, and opportunity. When you build it, no one can take it.

THE SIX STEPS TO BECOMING AN ASSET

Step One: Win on Repeat

Everyone has a rhythm for how they do life. It is their comfort zone, their unconscious moves that happen on repeat that led to their results. Some choose a rhythm to win, and some choose a rhythm to lose.

Are you winning on repeat? If not, you may be losing by default.

Winning is simply a choice to finish what you start, and it's possible to create a win daily. You can win the day by winning your morning. You can win your health by repeating a few small things like movement, water, and good nutrition. You can win your confidence by controlling what you think, say, and believe. Patterns repeated are what build your life's rhythms. Check your patterns, because you can win when you want to.

How are your patterns stacking up? Are you frustrated on repeat? Happy or sad on repeat? Winning or losing . . . or lost on repeat? What is your current rhythm of life?

Friends, please remember that the stars do not align for those who dabble. We must make big moves that matter to create a pattern we recognize enough to repeat. Ask yourself where would you like to win next: More money? More time? Better family life? Make the plan with the rhythms to win, then make no excuses.

When you can win the morning, you can win the day. When you can win the week and the month, your mind forgets how to lose and a new rhythm to win is born. Try it, you'll like it! Document the wins, focus there, and you may be shocked how quickly you can scale anything. You will make winning your go-to move!

Step Two: Work the Antidotes for Your Ugliness

Be clear (but gentle) that the ugly parts are no longer welcome here.

As you go for success, your growth is often very ugly. You are going to be introduced to the parts of yourself that need the most growth.

Every time I wanted to grow, I had to let go of a lesser part of me. My grandpa would always tell me, "If the world bumps you around a little bit, you probably had something to do with it." So I knew that my problems were just that—mine. No one to blame but my reactions, inadequacies, and need to learn a new way through every time I was challenged. Most people blame their lack of results on others, their problems on something from the past . . . they do anything to skip responsibility. And if it's not blame, it is self-deprecation. I'm not worth it, I'm not good enough—which is also a big load of crap. You woke up today worth it, so no more adult version of the-dog-ate-my-homework excuses. Call a spade a spade. I'm either ready to grow and I choose it, or I let my excuses hide me from success.

So here is how we do it: I take the pain and go all-in to working its opposite. If it's self-doubt tripping me up, I fill my house with sticky notes of belief and confidence, speak only words of love, and smile in the mirror two minutes a day while complimenting myself until I believe it. If it's laziness, I schedule big meetings that require my best. I wake earlier and prepare longer. I make the schedule make me work. Soon I get used to the new, and it's out with the old and in with the true! I worked the antidote until I became it. Sounds silly, but it works every time. Winning is faster than healing, and success is the new antidote.

Step Three: Get Mentored or Remain

People have asked, "How'd you do it so fast, Danelle?"

Well, the pain of losing was excruciating, so all I could do was learn faster than my competition. I read, studied, and earned until I could afford the best mentorship. Then when I could, I invested big so that my mentors were committed to help me and I was committed to make it work. I had to make the investment pay off.

If you look at why people lose or go slow, it's typically because they slow their learning process or don't put themselves in a situation where they must win. Accountability to someone who matters to you is what worked for me. I would be okay letting myself down, but I wasn't okay letting my kids, my mentors, or my clients who needed my best down. This one secret is what helped me accelerate faster than most, because I wasn't just committed to learning, but I was committed to the application of learning.

Have someone watch you that inspires and intimidates you, someone you would love to trade places with or do life and business with. When you find them, pay them to assist you, and work it like your results will honor them for the rest of your life. It will create incredible relationships, connections, and opportunities you never planned. Many of my mentors became my business partners because of how we were committed to growth.

Now some people will say, "I don't have to pay someone to get this", and I will remind you: no valuable human will give you their best for free even if they are incredibly generous. They will talk for free in their spare time because they have a great heart, but wouldn't you rather pay for the best information than gain just the casual kind? You don't want your life guidance based on information given in someone's spare time; you want their best mind. When people pay, everyone pays attention.

Step Four: Do It for You

Today's pressures of making life look perfect online have created many challenges for people looking to pursue more. For some, social pressures push perfection; for others, they push comparison and a filtered look at reality. This can often create distractions or take an entrepreneur just a little bit off course of their original mission, and soon they get lost in a sea of fake; or they don't like themselves, their work, and quit all together, killing what could have done massive good.

I encourage you to be so clear in your mission that in four words or less you can describe what you are fighting for every day. Maybe the goal is, "Leave people better than you found them," or maybe your mission is "To move lives forward," or help people "Take care of themselves." What your mission is and how you will deliver it every day will keep you in line.

Next, you must define your values, the three-to-four core characteristics you will operate with that will make it easy to say either yes to things that align, or no to things that don't. I always use my key phrase, "If in doubt, it's out." If you do it for you, the "'gram" will also reward it. "Fake it till you make it," is no longer an acceptable idea. If it's real, it's your deal.

Step Five: Keep Focused on Who Loses if You Don't Win

I've seen so many people pause their empire building because they cancel themselves. People question, doubt, and talk themselves out. This one method I use can change all of that.

Make a list of everyone your next goal or big win could help. Who would benefit most from your higher income and better opportunities? How would your customers be affected when they use your product they hadn't known about? Make the lists, and make it long. Then when you start to question, read that list and think about who you serve over yourself. You will start working in the right direction.

I got over my nerves by digging into my heart for who I could help. My kids, my friends, my connections—I wanted no one to lose on my watch. And when every day I started with who loses if I don't win right now, I started fighting for those I could help and stopped fighting against why I thought I couldn't. It is about what we give and who we help, not anything else.

So get it on paper. Who are you committed to help?

Step Six: Self Control Is Critical

Mastery of self is the secret sauce to influential success. There will be forces of good and evil along your road to win, but understand this: you develop a special kind of self-control in learning to win even while being cheated, mistreated, beat down, and embarrassed along the way. That human that has been up against the strongest of battles and challenges and comes through innovating and conquering with a smile. That human that has been cheated, hated, and mistreated, but has risen with complete self-control. No matter what the world throws their way, they simply seem ready, trained, and equipped for anything. That person, that winner, is who you would choose to rise with.

You must become the human in control enough to be brought into the world's biggest challenges because you can be counted on to finish with class. This piece is critical to becoming the one everyone can trust when something can only be done by a seasoned professional. When you don't give yourself the option to lose it or quit, then it will always be a winning season. You must know that every relationship counts, and every response and move matters. When you can control that, you can control your path.

It took me many years to learn the true art of wealth building, and the lessons I learned on this path allowed me to define who and what I needed to be. It made me an asset, and that has built me wealth that could never compare to just income: connections all over the world, respect from men and women in business, being one of the highest-ranked speakers and innovators for global brands and biggest strategists to help people earn, and the commitment to teaching others how to win big and massively give back. This is how you live for all as an asset. This is how you build and multiply your wealth.

Every step of the journey is about becoming the one you and everyone else can count on. It cannot be gifted. It can only be earned. Go become an asset and then true wealth, the unstealable kind, will be your gift.

— Danelle

CHAPTER 19

VISUALIZE SUCCESS

APRIL RYAN

—Founder and CEO of Red Iguana

I want to start by saying that 80 percent of my life is my work. From the earliest years of my life, I've gravitated toward the beauty industry. I've seen my successes before they came to life, all of them stemming from my soul's desire for more. More security. More wealth. More opportunities. Envisioning my success was not something that came easily to me. It was something I had to work hard for, and I learned many lessons along the way.

CALM INTROVERT

I come from a poor upbringing: born in Nadym, Russia, and raised in the small town of Salsk. My mother raised me to always explore my creative side. She always encouraged my artistic ventures most. I didn't have a lot of opportunities growing up poor, but that only helped me get more and more creative with whatever I had access to.

I initially started my journey in the beauty industry as a teenager taking cosmetology classes and learning from professional nail technicians. I was artistic growing up, much like my mom pushed me to be, but it wasn't long until I found my passion in business, nor was it long until I became a salon owner myself. I knew I could be more than just a regular nail technician, and opening my own salon was the next logical step for a nail tech who envisioned more for her life. I felt that

I could run a successful business, and I had enough knowledge and passion for it. When I opened my salon, it was the first nail salon in my city, and I was overflowing with happiness. Other salons had all types of beauty services, but I created something special. People knew my name and could trust not just me, but my business as well.

I soon realized I reached my business limits in Russia. I saw more opportunities in the United States, and eventually made my way there. Once in the US, I was able to really launch my business.

I am a huge introvert, so launching a business was scary for me. Being the face of a company, I had to push myself outside my introvert bubble. I like to gain self-knowledge through watching YouTube videos like John Kehoe's "Mind Power," and I like to read the likes of *The Secret* by Rhonda Byrne and *Today's Action, Tomorrow's Wealth* by Sam Rossi—the very book that educated me to get out of my introversion and how to talk to millionaires and various important heads in my industry. These self-enriching habits have allowed me to face some of my hardest days and reap my perpetual successes.

I want to share a small secret about how those hard days are conquered with positivity. For the most part, I like to think that much of my success is thanks to a hidden skill that anybody can tap into. It's called visualization.

VISUALIZATION RITUALS

You may have heard of it; visualization is closely associated with the law of attraction and manifesting. I guess I can say that I started visualizing at a young age when I was daydreaming about success and wealth, but the difference between visualizing and daydreaming is the intention aspect.

Incorporating visualization and manifestation rituals all started from a simple desire of mine. It's kind of funny when I think about it now, and it's something very small that I manifested so seamlessly. It was the simple idea of going to an expensive grocery store one day and never having to worry about the price of my favorite foods. As I grew up poor, I wanted to be in a situation where I could buy anything that I wanted without having to choose between one or the other. Today, I find myself in that very situation: I can purchase all options without having to choose or worry.

I intentionally visualize all the things that I want. I find that visualization works best when I'm in a meditative state, which can be anywhere from yoga, working out, or any activity that I feel most focused and raw. In the morning when I do my yoga, I start my visualization ritual by thinking of all the things that I am grateful for. I then mentally picture all the things that I want to bring into my life, whether that be a new car or my dream penthouse in New York City.

I like to incorporate mantras or confidence-boosting affirmations that can also be used if you ever find yourself having a tough time picturing things in your mind. For example, sometimes when I'm in the middle of my workout, I fixate on my own gaze in the mirror. With each bicep curl, I say to myself, "I am strong. I am unstoppable. I can achieve anything that I want." When we put our body in a state of physical activity, our mind becomes clearer and is able to plant new seeds. It can be as simple or specific as you'd like them to be. I like to repeat those positive self-talks over and over so they develop into positive thoughts, which eventually become a part of my conscious belief system. When we prioritize a positive daily mindset while also entertaining thoughts about the things we want, the brain creates ways to get it.

RED IGUANA

It's wild to think that the once young girl who was sitting amongst her classmates, creating mini-nail designs, visualized her success and grew up to be at the helm of a million-dollar beauty business. And it's not just any business—it's the very space that I've put my all into. I call it Red Iguana, cheekily named after my favorite pet.

Red Iguana uses high-quality ingredients in all our products, which is something I am very passionate about. It's my first rule because I found not many companies care about the harmful chemicals their customers are putting on their bodies. By considering the best ingredients for my people, Red Iguana has truly been able to break into a highly competitive market.

My company is also known for an invention that has allowed aspiring nail technicians around the globe to hone their skills. The idea came from personally experiencing the inconveniences of constantly asking someone to be a hand model to practice on. I pictured having a practice tool always at the ready, and so I figured the practical approach was to invent an instrument that nail technician trainees can use. This dream became Red Iguana's very own—and first on the market—Silicone

Practice Hand. This invention changed my business and revolutionized the nail industry on a worldwide scale. I wasn't expecting the success that came with the silicone hand; I was just looking for a more convenient way for technicians to hone their skills, myself included.

Before the success of the silicone hand, I utilized different methods for bringing money in: I created videos for nail companies, sold nail cuticle bits, and more. I created the silicone hand to make my work with videos easier, but it became the thing that brought the most money in. It's such a fantastic idea that many vendors produce dupes of my greatest invention, but that doesn't really bother me. Why? My customers, and the audience to which I cater, know that Red Iguana is the most real of real deals because we focus on quality over quantity. We use the best ingredients, the best silicone, and have good vibes. We provide great customer assistance and spread love, positivity, and support in all our social media accounts. When I was a young girl visualizing success in my life, these are all the ideas and emotions I knew I would need to find that success.

That's another thing that I do as a business owner: while creating and launching high-quality tools and products, I also create my own content and produce engaging visuals to interact with my audience. I show people Red Iguana's quality, which, in turn, helps manifest more opportunities and brand recognition for my work. It's my baby, so it's very important to build Red Iguana as a brand, and I've been fortunate to grow that name and high reputation immensely. I'm sure my brand is strong because many people call silicone hands—it doesn't matter what company they come from—the "Red Iguana Hand."

CAUTION: CUTTHROATS

A lot goes into building your success. One aspect of this process that is often overlooked or taken for granted is your support system. Taking the time to really envision what kind of people you want in your inner circle and then reflecting on who is genuine in their support for you and who is not will help you determine who to keep around when your business takes off. I learned some hard lessons stepping into the beauty industry. You can do your job perfectly but make little money. Someone can do a very average job but be on top in their business. Not every successful person is talented. A lot of them just have great communication skills and connections.

Moreover, I learned of the beauty industry's competitive nature, which is exciting to me and pushes me to work hard, but I've also seen what it can turn its community members into. Due to how cutthroat this industry can be, it can be hard to know who your friends are—who's going to be there to cheer you on through your successes, and who will secretly revel in your low moments when you need their advice. It's almost impossible for nail influencers to have a genuine relationship with nail companies. Most companies want to use you, your time, and your knowledge for free or for very little money. I know a lot of people who were treated poorly and weren't paid for their jobs. On the other hand, there are influencers who are paid by companies to leave good/bad reviews on products. This industry is full of drama, and I'm trying to stay away from it.

Fortunately, I have found companionship like no other with fellow beauty entrepreneur Analuisa Franklin. We're so close, so genuine, and so there for each other. It's real with her. She adds to both the business and personal sectors of my life. A true rockstar. Actions speak for themselves. A person can tell you they love you or support you, but those are just words. When they show you with their actions, unconditionally and unlimiting, that they love and support you, that's when you know they are genuine.

My beautiful and encouraging mother is another genuine support system I can lean on; I know she supports me in anything I do. Along with my mother, I have my amazing husband, Artem. He's so extroverted and energetic. Being around his energy inspires me to come out of my comfort zone. He helped me start Red Iguana and supported me by doing all the "boring" tasks such as registrations, taxes, licenses, etc., which allowed me to focus on the things I enjoy: product development, marketing, content creation, etc. Red Iguana wouldn't exist without him, and I'm forever grateful.

Maybe you are visualizing those people in your life right now and manifesting the relationships that you know will help you. We all need good friends and people to help us, champion us, and cheer us on.

When you're a celebrity in your industry, you communicate with a lot of people and learn how they act, so I have a strong sensitivity to people's vibes. Your experiences allow you to understand if the support you receive is genuine or fake from that very first interaction. Most people are not good enough actors to hide their true intentions. It's easy to understand when someone just wants to use your name and fame. When the person is right, you just feel it and think, "This is the one!" I cherish my support system, as they love me through my toughest moments and celebrate me on my milestone days.

PAST MY COMFORT ZONE

Not only have I found success in the business world with the Silicone Practice Hand and my brand recognition, but I also like to reflect on my personal successes as well. I have pushed myself to go beyond my comfort zone. It's been scary at times, almost to the point of making myself nauseous, but I've learned that the fear is all in my head. Every time I visualized and tried something new, even if it wasn't successful, my world didn't fall apart, my life didn't end, and no one was hurt. Yes, I lost some money on occasion, and I'm constantly surrounded by ungenuine people trying to discern their true intentions, but those aren't things I worry about. It was all worth it, however, because now I have Red Iguana.

During my life and through the experience of building of Red Iguana, I've uncovered some ideologies that I firmly stand by:

- When you go into business, you need to be fearless and visualize your success from the beginning. Try new things, take that risk.
- When you care about people's opinions, you are not putting yourself first. You can't make everyone happy, so focus on your own vision.
- When people are talking and imitating you, you're probably doing something right and your vision is sticking.

I find that this advice has always worked for me. By remembering these three things, I have filtered out the negativity and given my all to my business from my best and most-ample self. When I actively work to make myself forget that people's opinions exist, nothing changes in my business model, but my mental health becomes stronger. I'm always working—whether that be externally or internally. Working to better both my business and my personal life through the visualization of success has been key in finding my wealth.

— April

CHAPTER 20

SHOWING UP AS THE VIP OF YOUR OWN LIFE IN GRATITUDE

BARBIE LAYTON

—Host of the TV Channel You Are Amazing!

To me, wealth is synonymous with abundance, meaning that you have what you need when you need it and know that there is enough, and the more you have, the more you can share! This may come as a shock, but it is okay to have nice things! It is okay to indulge! For example, I have chocolate in my freezer from all over the world, and I realize that I don't crave chocolate because I understand that I can have it whenever I want, or when I do, I have one piece and savor it. When we want what we think we cannot have, it creates a scarcity mindset. Indulging in that thing you want occasionally is completely valid because doing so on occasion allows you to relax and enjoy it. It's healthier for our current and future selves to allow and accept the opportunities to feel good. When we allow those moments, our brain understands that we have great worth; this is amplified by what makes us feel good and we will naturally be engaged to bring more great things into our lives.

FAMILY MONEY TREE

I learned about an abundance mindset early on, growing up "wealth adjacent" in majestic Malibu, California. Having been surrounded by movie stars and fancy cars as just a regular kid, I can see the impact of my ancestors' lives on my perspective of wealth. The maternal side of my family originally came from wealth traced back to the 1300s that was taken during World War II, and they escaped with what they could carry. My grandmother spoke nine languages, and they were immigrants to two new countries. They saw all work as an opportunity and my grandfather even worked into his seventies.

On the other side of my family, my grandparents were originally from the Midwest, and my grandma was an Oklahoma beauty queen who met my grandfather during World War II at a bomb munitions plant. They had survived the Great Depression, so they were always very frugal, except when it came to the quality of food for holidays. My grandfather was friends with 1950s cowboy icon Hopalong Cassidy and Shirley Temple Black, and he cashed checks for Mae West as they thought she was an impersonator of herself! My parents met on the beach in Malibu, as my father was an OG surfer in the 1960s, and my mother was a cute blonde from Germany.

My mom was a genius at stretching a dollar! We used to go to garage sales in the wealthy neighborhoods in Malibu and get all kinds of things like art or tens of thousands of dollars' worth of designer shoes in a bag for twenty dollars! Consignment and thrift stores are still one of my favorite places. I had everything I wanted materially, even if it was last year's model. The phrase rings true: one woman's trash is another woman's treasure.

All things that you consider your wealth come from your own perspective. Our family always had the nicest things but at very discounted prices. I was told that although we lived in a beautiful home, we were the poorest kids on the block. So, we shared chores and did all our gardening ourselves, and I didn't have a maid like most of my friends did. I did most of the cooking, laundry, and shopping. I could also make a budget and it taught me responsibility. I was truly grateful for this perspective I was given.

EXTERIOR SHELL

Travel was my passion, and I love experiencing new cultures and learning new languages. I enjoyed two international trips a year, lived on three continents, visited over thirty-five countries, most of the United States, and the Hawaiian Islands. When I was diagnosed with excruciating and incurable Crohn's disease back in 2016, I started using fashion as a form of therapy. This coping strategy saved me. Before that diagnosis, I had already survived three near-death experiences and yet continued to be active. At that time, I was single and working every day, and after work, I was homebound on the couch with an ice pack due to intense sharp pain. Sometimes it was so intense that I made my fashion therapy into a formula. There were days when my pain and low energy would make me feel horrible, and I intentionally chose fashion that could be red carpet worthy. It would help me feel like I could make it through the day, and I would find myself feeling better. It is very satisfying to do my makeup and put on an outfit that makes me feel good occasionally, but being intentional about it daily made a huge difference.

I started experimenting with different styles, wigs, makeup, and designer brands. I was pulled toward amplifying my exterior shell because I realized that when you're faced with your own mortality and the belief that you might die soon, you see that you've kept all the good stuff locked away. It's like when you visit your grandmother's house and there are plastic sheets over the "good" furniture to keep them in pristine condition, but she never genuinely enjoys the luxury herself. What's the point of having a couch if you don't allow yourself to sit on the comfortable cushion? I took this instance and ran in the opposite direction.

VIP MINDSET

I figured then that if I was going to die, I might as well enjoy my wealth while I was alive. Since I dressed intentionally, I would be fully decked out on a Tuesday, and when I went to Costco, I would find I would suddenly have a personal shopper, or I would get an extra VIP experience or bonuses when I showed up like that at restaurants. It was such an uncanny thing that people were serving me in such a beautiful way, and I was so grateful as it was a different way to be received.

I landed upon an empowering perspective: you are the VIP of your own life. You are the person that should be pulling out the best perfume and the best China set and not saving it for show. I imagine money as an energy, and it's something you can play with. When you continue to think in a scarcity mindset, you will only go in that direction. However, this is an unlimited universe with abundant resources, and there's enough for everybody depending on what you want. I'm very big on shifting your mindset, and we inspire the wealth that comes our way. It's like flying at the airport. I didn't even know there were VIP lounges in airports, but when you gain access, they have fabulous amenities, smoked glass, and no signs. It's like magical doors are opening for you that you never even knew existed! A lot of it centers around gratitude. I was grateful for the airport before, but by shifting my mindset to being my own VIP, I found the world upgraded for me!

GAMIFICATION

Then, in 2017 when I was in a lot of pain, I remember seeing a host on MTV's *Total Request Live* wearing a Louis Vuitton x Supreme jacket, and I admired it. Somebody told me it costs $6,000, which was absurd to me, but then through further educating myself, I understood that streetwear became a subculture; people were waiting in lines to get a taste. It was literally like its own language. I was so intrigued, I started doing something I call *gamification*: I essentially made finding and buying certain designer gems into my own little game. To some, this may sound silly, but it gave me something to live for and added some sweetness and joy back into my life. Often, manifestation is about suspending disbelief and stepping into childlike wonder. It's like being a five-year-old on Christmas morning and it changes your whole vibe!

Although I love to look my best, my messages are never about perfection. Being a naturally curvy woman, designer clothes were out of reach when I was younger, as they didn't make my size, nor could I afford them. Being able to find them at a bargain or on sale in my size made for an extra special fun treat. I always tell people, "You are your own reality show." It's about showing up for yourself and manifesting opportunities for you to enjoy life to the fullest. These ideas certainly contributed to saving my life, because from this perspective, I felt like I had everything I needed, and I was able to manifest the rest.

During the pandemic, audiences of The Best You Expos responded positively to what I call Extreme Gratitude. I had people messaging me that it kept them calm and preserved their sanity, as it was such an easy refrain. I told people to thank their car, toilet, shower, stove, sink, bed, the roof over their head—you name it. I also asked them to thank the electric company and internet providers who are keeping the lights on and allowing them to work from home. There was a dramatic shift in perspective when people stacked up about twenty things for which they have gratitude! They didn't sit around complaining about what they didn't have because they were able to focus on the multiple people and things that are supporting their livelihood and their ability to do what they need to do. We have to start with gratitude for where we are in this very moment and build from there!

SERVICE MINDSET

What I learned growing up gave me a strong foundation of hard work and gratitude. As a kid, I was service-oriented, and as a teen, I volunteered at Los Niños Children's Charity in Tijuana, Mexico. I put my heart into other community service projects, and this continued into adulthood. I volunteered at the animal shelter and spent five years at my university reading grad papers to help support its mission of spiritual psychology. Working hard, doing what I had to do, and looking for ways to help others along the way, I always wanted to add value to my communities and enrich others. I think the biggest gift to give the world is simply living and being authentically you, because there is wealth in presenting the truest version of yourself. When you do acquire all kinds of wealth, whether tangible or immaterial, it won't mean a thing if you don't pay it forward. When we believe in the power that is in the reciprocity of giving and operate from the purity of service, generosity, and giving for giving's sake, that is wealth in its most exalted form. Money for money's sake is hollow, whereas money in service to yourself and to benefit others multiplies.

Now, I host the program *You Are Amazing!* on the Best You TV, which has brought together twenty countries in participating in my Kindness Revolution. The Kindness Revolution's mission is to dispel stereotypes and honor each person's journey, one heart at a time. It's about finding common ground without media-influenced narratives and to bring forth stories and discussions that are authentic, empowering, and ultimately relatable. I believe in the power of unity through kindness, especially amongst women. When women band together without competing and lift each other up from the heart space, they can be so powerful. It's in the collaboration and co-creation where we can positively change and truly come through for one another.

In Maslow's hierarchy of needs, there is something we all have in common: needing to be seen, heard, loved, and accepted. With clients, I keep that at the forefront because everybody wants and needs the same things. As an intuitive consultant, mentor, and speaker, I help people fall in love with themselves by reflecting their internal beauty back to them. I show them how to tap into their flow of abundant energy, their worth, their abilities, and all of the love within their grasp to level-up their life.

I think of myself as a heart-centered conscious entrepreneur and speak to everyone as my equal. Although I may dress up and present as an important person, I thank people who help me and ask people how their day is going because approaching with kindness is a priceless act. Kindness also gives people the opportunity to reciprocate it back to you. My goal in the Kindness Revolution was inspired by one of my favorite mantras: the more I have, the more I can share. My goal is to continue accessing large global spaces and networks to bring my wisdom and inspire the masses. I value being able to connect with different communities and cultures.

My show was originally born out of honoring my mentors, like Vishen Lakhiani and Naveen Jain, who encouraged me to be bold and Ken Honda, the Zen Millionaire who talks about happy money, clearing money wounds, and thanking the money that you give and get. Today, when I pay my bills or have money come in, I say, "Thank you!" He calls it the *Arigato* In and *Arigato* Out, and it's all about thanking everything you have and staying in the gratitude frequency, which has been scientifically measured. Manifestation occurs above 528 Hz,[1] which magnetizes it back to you in a flow where you feel like you can have whatever you want, and it resonates at the same wavelength as you receive it. I hope you find your own definition of wealth and step into your own greatness. Go ahead—what is in your closet that you've been saving to wear someday? Get it out and enjoy it. You're worth it!

—BARBIE

NOTES:

1. "Solfeggio Frequency Guide," Solfeggio Guide (September 30, 2019). https://solfeggioguide.com/solfeggio-frequency-guide/

CHAPTER 21

BRAND CURRENCY WEARS THE CROWN

RHONDA SWAN

—International Bestselling Author, Founder and CEO of Unstoppable Branding Agency and WILD Magazine, and TV Host of The Rhonda Swan Show

I was born in Detroit, Michigan, to young parents: my father, a drifter and addict, and my mom a twenty-year-old that did her best to keep me out of harm's way from my father's volatile mood swings. I frequently stayed with my mom's parents. Granny was a stay-at-home mom, and my Paw a blue-collar, union factory worker.

When I was five, my mom remarried to my stepdad, a fireman and entrepreneur. He brought stability and showed me what it meant to work hard and be proud of what you do, no matter how small. But the word "wealth" in my household was synonymous with money and held a negative connotation—the root of all evil, as the saying goes.

I don't fault my parents for their belief system; it's what they were brought up with and what their parents learned. These kinds of mindsets are passed down from generation to generation by our parents without them even knowing the damage it can have on a young person's ability to make their own judgements or decisions on what wealth means to them, and to understand that wealth doesn't have to be only about money. When I graduated from university and continued on to my master's degree, I thought that the most important goal was to get a high-paying job with benefits, an IRA, stock options, and insurance so that I could start building my future. There was no foundation for me to believe that wealth could come from many other areas in my life. And this kind of thinking will continue to pass down throughout your family lineage until one day, someone decides to change it.

Needless to say, I didn't grow up with a foundation or knowledge of what wealth could mean other than "money," let alone understand how to create or accumulate nontraditional wealth, but I was determined to find it and change the mindset that was passed down to me.

Over the last forty-nine years of my life I have been a student. Every decade that passed, the definition of wealth was being refined and redefined. I have attended over two-hundred-plus personal development events and entrepreneurial events, absorbing their wisdom and guidance for creating a fulfilled life so that I could rewrite the definition of wealth handed down to me. I would ask the speakers what their definition of wealth and success was; most of them never started with money. It was joy, fulfillment, honesty, integrity, freedom, memories, and relationships that were at the forefront of their replies. I started to realize that it wasn't the money that made these people successful or wealthy, it was their core values and what they perceived wealth to be.

THE DEFINING MOMENT

In 2004, I showed up to a Monday morning business meeting and watched a woman put her newborn baby in daycare so she could go back to work. At that moment, I made a conscious decision that I was going to quit my corporate job so that I could raise a family and not put my baby in daycare.

I'll be honest, I had no idea what I would do to make money, but I knew I couldn't continue down this path. We were living the "*Keeping Up with the Joneses*" kind of life. Brian and I had just bought a five-bedroom home in San Diego to start a family, so when I came home and told him I was quitting my job, he almost passed out.

"I don't care if you're my boss's boss's boss, I'll never make enough money to cover the mortgage of this house on my salary," he said.

"Fine, I'll figure it out. I'm going to work online," I quickly replied with my Detroit Girl attitude.

Little did he know, I had just finished watching a documentary about Steve Jobs that stressed leveraging the internet or, in the next ten years, you'll be in the dark. I took that statement seriously and started learning the power of online branding, Google AdWords, SEO, target marketing, and storytelling from some of the greatest teachers in the world.

I spent days, nights, and weekends learning everything I could. I was determined to build a business, leave my job, and raise a child on my terms, but I didn't know it was going to be the hardest thing I would ever do. Brian was not supportive, thinking I was crazy for leaving a six-figure job; my friends called me irresponsible following a trend that would die in months. But I knew if I didn't do it now, I would never do it.

So I started searching for ways to put my new marketing education and skills into action. I found a network marketing company that sold personal development products and events that I could resell and make a commission on every sale.

I would sit in my office each day and call leads that would come in from my marketing. I was so determined to make my business work. I was placing three-line ads in newspapers, Google Ads, putting up signs on the windshield of people's cars in parking lots, posting up coroplast signs on the side of road. You name it; I did it all.

I had no shame, and everything to gain. In the first six months of starting my business, I called three thousand leads and didn't make a sale! Yes, that's three thousand leads! At this point I think most people would put their tail between their legs and go back to their job, but I knew I could do it. If others were able to make this business work, then I could too. I stayed focused and, within thirty days, I broke through, had a $47,000 month, and continued to grow and learn.

I not only quit my corporate job within the first year of building my business and brand online, but I made enough money for Brian to quit his job working as a robotics engineer. That was in 2004, and I've never looked back. Since then, we have been building our brands and business structures completely online while traveling the world.

THE VALUE OF BRAND CURRENCY

Most of us today understand what a brand is and associate it with a company or a product, but have you ever considered that your personal name or reputation could hold value or be considered currency? Well, I'm here to tell you that your Brand Currency can become your company's greatest asset. Think about it: our name, track record of success, reputation, and list of accomplishments is the strongest and most long-lasting currency you can have anywhere in the world. I have personally leveraged investment capital based on my name alone and no one ever pulled a credit report. I have accessed opportunities that ended up being priceless, and I never filled out any kind of application.

This is how I was offered to be the host of *New to the Street Unstoppable Show*, a TV segment that is filmed at NASDAQ MarketSite in New York City. Getting this show had everything to do with my brand's credibility, core values, and presence online.

I was in the USA for a month-long book tour. We had several events in Las Vegas, Los Angeles, and New York City where we launched our Times Square billboard. The producers of the show were looking for a woman CEO to host the new segment, and someone heard about the *Women Gone Wild* book launch and saw our billboard in Times Square and said, "You need to meet this woman that is leading the charge for this book. She would be perfect for your show host." The producers Googled my name and saw articles, videos, and the strength of my brand online and decided to reach out to me. Within forty-eight hours we were at dinner, discussing the details of the show.

Let's talk more deeply about how you can start creating and leveraging your brand as currency. This can be as simple as your reputation and how easy it is to access someone of high status because of your reputation. It can be your rolodex of contacts, feature articles that are written about you, testimonials from clients, endorsements from public figures, social proof pictures, or proof of results you have achieved or helped others achieve.

The perceived value of your reputation can be based on your accomplishments, but more importantly, your ability to make things happen in the world. The closest most people get to understanding this is with their CVs or resumes. But they sell themselves short when they do this. Giving someone a resume allows them to judge whether they think you are credible or not because all they are looking at are your experiences, but when you can highlight or leverage what others are saying about you in a testimonial or in an article, this gives you third-party validation of what you have done for them or someone else. This speaks louder than any CV or resume.

This is only the tip of the iceberg of how far your Brand Currency can take you since 90 percent of entrepreneurs and companies have no brand authority online—when someone searches their name, they are underneath the waterline and out of sight. Building your brand's online presence from the start of your career is vital in today's environment.

IMPORTANCE OF BRAND CORE VALUES

When I first launched my company, I focused on teaching people how to build their online brand presence and know what they stand for. This became finding the core values of a brand, which allow clients to know if they align with you and what you stand for—rather similar to dating.

Core brand values guide a brand's story, action, behaviors, and decision-making processes. They will be your guiding light when you have to make tough choices and will keep customers because they will believe in your brand. To do this, you need strong and easily understood values.

What brand values are right for your business? For most people, the first values that occur to them are rather vague: quality and reliability stand out quickly as brand values that most businesses can get behind, but you need to take it a bit further. By explaining just how your business embodies these values, you can better distinguish why it is an essential part of your company's core.

Considering a wide range of brand values can help you to determine just how to break down your business brand value into themes that you can incorporate into every aspect of your business. A list of values is a great way to brainstorm what is essential to your brand mission. If your mind goes to quality, consider values like accuracy, attention to detail, consistency, craftsmanship, excellence, expertise, and precision. On the other hand, if you want to express customer service, look at values like accessibility, approachability, care, communication, customer-centric, dependability, and empathy. Most business owners know how important it is for a brand to be consistent and distinct, but many people don't realize how vital brand value is to every aspect of their company When you establish your brand's core values from the start, it will give it form and make it easier for a customer to choose you.

RELATIONSHIPS FOR THE WIN

At its heart, branding and public relations are about building and managing relationships. It's important to keep strong relationships with customers, peers, influencers, or anyone that may be able to refer clients to you. You won't go wrong if you build relationships everywhere, with everyone, every time. Powerful relationships with all stakeholders make it easier for you to shape the public perception of your brand.

In our company we implemented the ABR rule—Always Building Relationships. It doesn't matter if you are online or working a job or building a brick-and-mortar business, relationships can take you further than any form of marketing.

Powerful connections with customers mean they will be loyal to your brand and tell their friends about you (free word-of-mouth marketing). Good relationships with journalists mean they will gladly cover your brand or pick you over another brand for a mention or even feature your story. Having favorable relationships with your community or other communities mean they will back you during a crisis and be willing to share what you do to their audience. Beneficial relationships with peers in your niche mean they will support all your branding initiatives. Good relationships are the linchpin of positive perspectives about your brand. It's never too late or too early to build relationships with all stakeholders who are key to the growth of your brand.

So, build relationships—now and forever. Your brand will be better for it.

— *RHONDA*

About the Authors

RHONDA SWAN is the founder and CEO of the Unstoppable Branding Agency, one of the top ten public relations and branding firms for entrepreneurs rated by *Forbes* magazine in 2021. She is also the founder of the international bestselling book series for women empowerment, Women Gone Wild and *WILD Magazine*. Rhonda was the TV cohost of *New to the Street Unstoppable Show*, flimed at NASDAQ Marketsite and can be seen on Fox Business and Newsmax, and as a sponsored program on Bloomberg TV. She also hosts *The Rhonda Swan Show*, which ris streamed to over one-million viewers per episode. She interviews entrepreneurs, changemakers, and public figures. Guests have included Grant Cardone, Elena Cardone, Kevin Harrington, Diana Wentworth, Tito Ortiz, and John Lee Dumas.

For her work and dedication, Rhonda has landed coverage in print and broadcast outlets around the world, and has been featured in *Forbes, Entrepreneur, Inc. Magazine, Success, Business Insider*, ABC, CBS, NBC, CNN, and *BuzzFeed*.

DIANA VON WELANETZ WENTWORTH is a *New York Times* bestselling author, renowned keynote speaker, and certified life coach specializing in reinvention. She has written award-winning books, including *Chicken Soup for the Soul Cookbook: 101 Stories with Recipes from the Heart, Send Me Someone: A True Story of Love Here and Hereafter, The Von Welanetz Guide to Ethnic Ingredients: How to Buy and Prepare More Than 1,000 Foods from Around the World*, and *The Pleasure of Your Company*, which received the R.T. French Tastemaker Cookbook of the Year award. As a lifetime entrepreneur, she hosted a long-running television series with her late husband Paul von Welanetz and founded the Inside Edge (www. InsideEdge.org), a weekly breakfast-speaker forum in Southern California that helped launch the careers of many celebrated authors and transformational speakers over the past thirty-five years. With her business partner, Robin Mullin, she launched Wisdom Circles, which provides women of exceptional mastery with ongoing meetings to explore topics such as reinvention, legacy, and the highest potential for their personal "Encore."

ADRIANA MONIQUE ALVAREZ is the CEO and Founder of AMA Publishing. She teaches women how to start highly profitable publishing companies and has written *How to Start a Six Figure Publishing Company* that is available on Amazon. She's a *USA Today* bestselling author and her most recent book *The Younger Self Letters* debuted number one on bestseller lists internationally. She has been seen in *Forbes, Huffington Post, International Living, America Daily Post, Daily Grind, Addicted2Success, Elephant Journal, London Daily Post, Entrepreneur*, Fox, ABC, and NBC. She is currently living in the middle-of-nowhere Colorado where she is renovating her grandparents' home and learning how to homestead with her husband Derek and two sons, Sam and Grant.

MICHELLE BELTRAN is a bestselling author of *Take the Leap: What It Really Means to be Psychic*, and is a globally celebrated intuitive expert, transformation trailblazer, and spiritual teacher. She has become a leading international authority in the spirituality arena specializing in psychic functioning, mediumship, and remote viewing. Having appeared at numerous spirituality and wellness summits, in magazines like *USA Today*, *Forbes*, and *Hay House World Summit*, and hosting a popular psychic development podcast, *The Intuitive Hour: Awaken Your Inner Voice*, she has worked with thousands of people across the globe. Michelle's greatest joy is seeing people engage in more fulfilling lives and teaching them how to awaken, amplify, and trust their inner voice. Currently, Michelle is based in Northern California. When she is not deeply immersed in authoring her next engaging read, you'll find her dancing the West Coast Swing to the current jams of the day or on her Orbea, summiting the biggest mountain she can find.

STEFANIE BRUNS is a quantum psychologist, business mentor, mother of four, and the founder and CEO of Business Flow Academy. With over twenty years' experience coaching ultra-successful people using methods that others would call crazy and spiritual, Stefanie is an expert in leading high performers and world leaders to more life force, energy, and success to achieve outstanding results and experiences. Her teachings, healings, and mentoring are like magical antidotes from the womb of the galaxy. Renowned for creating rapid shifts within the energetic fields of her clients and their businesses, her work is internationally appreciated in *Forbes*, *Influencive*, *Disrupt*, *The Entrepreneur*, *Daily Star*, *Hollywood Digest*, and more.

DANELLE DELGADO'S journey started with her raising three kids on her own, working three jobs, struggling to survive. Now, she has award-winning success in business and is a multi-entrepreneur known as the Millionaire Maker. She is the CEO of Life Intended LLC and the Internal Alliance, a known online influencer, international speaker, and author of the bestselling book *I Choose Joy*. Her training academy guides entrepreneurs both online and offline to scale their companies to a million and their lives to fulfillment. Whether training solopreneurs to large corporations, Danelle delivers results—fast. As one of the most sought-after female speakers and corporate trainers on marketing, sales, online business strategy, communication, and personal development in the world, she has been highlighted in *Forbes*, *USA Today*, *Entrepreneur*, and more. Outside of her work, Danelle spends time with her kids in Colorado, teaching them to live the life they are capable of just as she does with her clients.

MICHALE GABRIEL is a Parent's Choice award-winning performer, best-selling author, and founder/CEO of Story by Design. She is a story shaper, inspirational keynote speaker, leadership consultant, storytelling coach, and workshop facilitator. Her corporate clients include the Boeing Company, Infoblox, and Western Union. She founded the Young Storytellers for Peace US/USSR Program—which was the subject of an award-winning, nationally aired PBS documentary *Young Storytellers in Russia*—and Teachers for Peace USSR Program. She starred in a Russian-produced television storytelling series that promoted intercultural understanding to fifty million viewers during the Cold War, earning her the title of "Russia's American Fairy Godmother." Michale also founded the Storytelling Residency Program at Seattle Children's Hospital, and the Tell Me A Story Program in rural Alaska. She serves on nonprofit boards in Costa Rica and loves traveling, reading, experiencing cultures and cuisines, and exploring spirituality.

CAMBERLY GILMARTIN has always loved the written word. Her BA in English Literature and Writing from University of South Florida and MBA from Seattle University have facilitated a rewarding career in marketing and branding. At Curious Ant Creative, Camberly crafts brand and product stories and business strategy to increase visibility and revenue for businesses. As an entrepreneur, businesswoman, author, and parent, Camberly has been featured on *The Rhonda Swan Show* and in *Inc. Magazine*, *The Seattle Times*, *Total Girl Boss*, *Disrupt Magazine*, *So Influential*, and *The Hollywood Digest*. She has also appeared as a podcast guest to share the experiences and tools she has discovered along the way, to inspire others to live healthy, connected, joy-filled lives. When not writing, you will find Camberly in nature, with her family, friends, and pets. She lives in the Pacific Northwest where she has perfected the art of making her own sunshine. Gratitude is the frequency she lives on.

ANIA HALAMA is a world traveler who once worked a corporate job, living paycheck to paycheck; after a leap of faith, she began her journey of self-discovery. Now a spiritual life/business mentor and intuitive digital artist, she has helped thousands of heart-centered entrepreneurs attract wealth. She hosts the *Spirituality for Badass Babes* Podcast and cofounded Project Save the Toads. Ania is also an intuitive healer, Reiki Master, angel healer, EFT and *Ho'oponopono* master, Akashic records reader, and law of attraction coach. *Entrepreneur* listed her as a Top Millennial Powerhouse, and the *US Reporter* named her one of the top ten entrepreneurs to follow. She has spoken on international stages and has been featured in media, including *Yahoo News, New York Weekly Times, LA Weekly, Brainz Magazine, So Influential,* and others. Ania uses her eye for beauty, knowledge of business, and love of self-discovery to impact as many lives as possible.

DANA KAY is a board-certified holistic health and nutrition practitioner, two-time international bestselling author, and the CEO and founder of the ADHD Thrive Institute. As a mother of a child with ADHD, she knows firsthand the struggles that come with parenting a neurodiverse child and the freedom that is possible once parents learn to reduce ADHD symptoms. Dana has been featured in *Forbes* and *Authority Magazine* and on Medium, Influencive, Thrive Global, and various other media. She has also been a guest at multiple parenting and ADHD summits and podcasts. Her mission is to help families reduce ADHD symptoms naturally so that children with ADHD can thrive at home, at school, and in life.

BARBIE LAYTON is an international speaker and energy healer. Based on fan feedback and decades of speaking engagements, she graces places from international main stages to four giant New York Times Square billboards. She earned her MA in spiritual psychology from the University of Santa Monica and is a graduate of Vishen Lakhiani's MindValley Premium Coaching. She has a global TV channel called *You Are Amazing!* where she interviews world thought leaders. Her work has helped CEOs and individuals alike reanimate their dreams, fall in love with themselves, and become the VIP of their lives. Barbie also has multiple media appearances, such as the Cannes Film Festival winning documentary, *The Prison Project* (2007), as a counselor to women serving life sentences. She has been featured in *USA Today, Forbes,* and others. She spoke at the Think and Grow Rich world tour and the Los Angeles Tribune Neuroscience Summit, and is featured in *Hoinser Groups Queens* 2022 book and Dr. John De Martini's 2023 documentary, *Breakthrough*.

SHAR MOORE is a recognized talk show host of *The Girlfriend Hour TV*, award-winning mentor, bestselling author, speaker, and founder of the Feminessence® movement. She appears regularly in the media, with features in the *Daily Mail* and on *Studio 10, 7NEWS, 9News, MSN, WIN News, Mamamia*, Oprah.com, *Ninemsn, ABC Local Radio, 2SM*, and many other outlets. She is the number one bestselling author of *From Broke to BMW in 18 months: Your Step By Step Guide to Breaking Through Your Barriers To Achieve The Life You Deserve* and *Your Life Your Purpose: Your Step-by-Step Guide to Awakening Your Life's Purpose and Fulfilling Your Deepest Desires*. She has been awarded the Gold International Stevie award, the Woman of the Decade in Personal Leadership award, and the Queensland Business Excellence award. When she isn't preparing to be in the swag bags at the Oscars in 2023, she is continuing her global mission of guiding women to be seen, heard, and remembered.

ROBIN MULLIN is the Founder and CEO of Wisdom Circles LLC, launched in 2022. Her mission is to amplify the impact of conscious leaders by providing a spiritual community of high frequency collaborators, including intimate online groups, retreats, mentoring, and circle-facilitator training. A visionary leader who is passionate about building cultures and communities that foster creativity, collaboration, and collective wisdom, Robin's MA in organizational leadership led to teaching at Chapman University as an adjunct professor. She has held senior leadership roles in corporate and nonprofit organizations and served as the president of the Inside Edge Foundation for Education for several years. Robin is an enthusiastic *Oma* who delights in creating adventures for her *grands*. She loves reading poetry, crafting collages, and hosting themed dinner parties. Robin lives in San Clemente, California, where she strolls the nature trails with her fluffy dog, Alo.

KORTNEY MURRAY is one of the most connected female business leaders on the East Coast. After opening and, ultimately, closing her first business—a clothing boutique in San Diego—she moved into finance to help other small business owners, like herself, face the enormous challenge of navigating the financial world. As her knowledge of the industry grew, she formed her own company, Farhat Leasing LLC in 2007, which became the springboard for her current company, Coastal Kapital LLC. Kortney has been featured on NASDAQ, Newsmax, Bloomberg, Fox Business, and in magazines such as *USA Today*, *Forbes*, *Entrepreneur*, *LA Tribune*, *Think and Grow Rich*, and many more. She also sits on the board of American Association of Commercial Finance Brokers (AACFB). Kortney and her husband Chris are yoga instructors, the proud owners of four rescue felines, avid travelers and boaters, and rally for many charitable causes, most recently for autism spectrum disorders and cancer research.

TARRYN REEVES is a *USA Today* bestselling author, book coach, publisher, and marketer whose work has been featured in the *Los Angeles Times*, World News Network, Thrive Global, and more. Known as the "Book Queen," she is the CEO of Four Eagles Publishing, the publishing house of choice for conscious disruptors, visionaries, and leaders. Together with her team, she works with high-level entrepreneurs to create bestselling books that act as marketing tools and authority builders, promote growth in businesses, and create ripple effects across the globe with their messages. Tarryn is also a highly sought-after speaker and freelance writer working with some of the top PR agencies in the world to craft words that move people. Originally from Zimbabwe, Tarryn now lives in Australia. When she isn't writing, Tarryn can be found adventuring the globe, reading a good book, or dancing in her kitchen.

APRIL RYAN was born in Nadym, Russia. She began her career as a nail technician at the age of eighteen. Currently thirty-four years old, she is the CEO of Red Iguana, one of the most well-known nail brands that makes all their products with high-quality ingredients. April invented the globally popular Silicone Practice Hand for nail technicians, which have been a game-changer in the industry. April also has a heart for helping people and participating in charity activities.

GENEVIEVE SEARLE, The Optimization Queen, has spoken on the TEDx Talk stage with, "How to Thrive in an Era of Uncertainty." This WILD woman mentors game-changing women to align with their genetic genius so they can actualise their Soul Purpose. Genevieve combines cutting-edge epigenetic profiling, ancestral alchemy, embodied movement, functional breathing, and deep soul work. She is also the Amazon number one bestselling author of *Embrace Your Feminessence: A Must Read for Every Woman Who Wants to Embrace Their Power* and *Illuminate Your Feminessence*. Working with Genevieve comes with the warning, "Enter at your own risk. You will not be the same woman after working with me." When she isn't speaking on massive stages, she can be found dancing, writing poetry, being a conscious mother to her three sons, ally to her lover of over twenty years, and generally being fabulous.

HANALEI SWAN is a fifteen-year-old fashion designer, artist, model, international speaker, and bestselling author. At the age of seven, she discovered her talents, and the journey began. Her parents never asked her, "What do you want to be when you grow up?" Rather, they asked her, "What do you want to be right now?" This question sparked her career as a fashion designer, and today, Hanalei is one of the youngest fashion designers and business owners in the world, producing high-fashion, life- and earth-conscious products out of her showroom in Bali, Indonesia. She has spoken on stages in Australia, Hong Kong, India, London, Indonesia, and across America, inspiring people to act on their dreams. Hanalei's mission focuses on inspiring the next generation of conscious leaders to do what they love while keeping the earth and their global impact in mind. She released her book *How to Be & Raise an UNSTOPPABLE Kid* in January 2019.

EBONY SWANK is the founder and CEO of Swank A Posh, a women's clothing boutique. After a brief, failed first launch in 2009, Ebony had to go back to the drawing board and quickly realized there was a gap in the market for long, stretchy jeans that women felt confident wearing. She then created jeans in multiple styles, mastered her target customer, and invested her last $12,000 into a new store, which has grown into an eight-figure establishment.

Swank A Posh is known for their stretchy SuperGa Jeans, trendsetting fashion, and infamous try-on videos. Her company has multiple locations in the Metro Detroit area and a massive online following.

Ebony has been able to employ young black women with entry-level experience and mentor them to executives; she single-handedly aids women to be confident in their own skin. Swank has been featured in *Forbes, Business Deccan, Rolling Out, Black Enterprise,* and countless other publications.

BLAIR KAPLAN VENABLES is an expert in social media marketing and the president of Blair Kaplan Communications, a British Columbia-based PR agency. She is the creator of the Social Media Empowerment Pillars, has helped customers grow their followers into the tens of thousands in just one month, and has won integrative marketing awards. *USA Today* named Blair as one of the Top 10 Conscious Female Leaders to Watch in 2022, and her expertise has been featured in *Forbes, CBC Radio, Entrepreneur,* and *Thrive Global.* She is an Amazon bestselling author for her books *Pulsing Through My Veins: Raw and Real Stories From An Entrepreneur* and *The Global Resilience Project* book. Blair's passion is growing the Global Resilience Project's community, where users share their stories of overcoming life's most difficult moments.

KAREN WHELAN is a transformational psychotherapist, intuitive consultant, Tantra teacher, Rising Star healer, Workshop Women Gone Wild facilitator, retreat leader, and international bestselling author as well as a self-published author of two memoirs. Karen is the founder of Soulution Therapy, which offers transformative services to companies, individuals, groups, couples, and teenagers. Karen has worked with clients for over fourteen years and has witnessed thousands of clients transform their lives. Her work has allowed her to sit with world experts like Dr. Joe Dispenza, Gabor Maté (while training in Living Inquiries), and the incredible spiritual teacher, humanitarian, and wellness expert Derek O'Neill. Karen's work has earned her invitations and coverage on TV and radio shows. She has written for a monthly wellness column, served as a keynote speaker at the Women Gone Wild Summit in 2021, and has been featured in *Forbes, USA Today, Los Angeles Weekly Times, Hollywood Digest, Yahoo News, Thrive Global,* and other outlets.